THE MATHEMATICAL REVOLUTION IN
SOVIET ECONOMICS

The
Mathematical Revolution
in Soviet Economics

ALFRED ZAUBERMAN

Published for
THE ROYAL INSTITUTE OF INTERNATIONAL AFFAIRS
by
OXFORD UNIVERSITY PRESS
LONDON   NEW YORK   TORONTO
1975

Oxford University Press, Ely House, London W1

GLASGOW NEW YORK TORONTO MELBOURNE WELLINGTON
CAPE TOWN IBADAN NAIROBI DAR ES SALAAM
LUSAKA ADDIS ABABA DELHI BOMBAY CALCUTTA
MADRAS KARACHI LAHORE DACCA KUALA LUMPUR
SINGAPORE HONG KONG TOKYO

ISBN 0 19 218303 6

Set in 11pt Photon Times, printed by photolithography,
and bound in Great Britain at The Pitman Press, Bath

To my wife

The title of this essay by the dean of Western students of Soviet economic thought is aptly chosen, for it deals with a veritable scientific revolution of great potential importance in the realm of practical affairs. With that masterful economy of strokes which betrays many years of dedicated effort, the author paints for the non-specialist reader a vivid picture of the impressive accomplishments and extreme travails of mathematical economics in the Soviet period. He concentrates on its phoenix-like resurgence since the late 'fifties, which is the 'revolution' of the title. He tells of the high hopes that attended the early days of that resurgence, hopes of translating the bright new corpus of theory into cornucopian planning practice, and of the inevitable transition to more sober estimates that followed. And he surely is correct in appraising developments since the late 'fifties as a return of Soviet economics into the mainstream of world economics, from which it had been forcibly wrenched by Stalin.

It is not impossible that even without the intrusion of mathematics Soviet economics would – sooner or later – have returned to that mainstream, which at its core is after all primarily a rational calculus of choice. Such concepts as the economic optimum, equilibrium, opportunity cost (for which there still seems to be no phrase in the Russian language), and the economic margin, would have eventually penetrated Soviet economic thought owing to the sheer force of the logic, despite the traditional hostility of orthodox Soviet economics to them. From these and related concepts a body of quite 'standard' theorems and propositions would have necessarily followed. The imperatives of detailed planning would have seen to it – sooner or later. But it was mathematics which supplied the irresistible weapons that (once the political barriers were raised) swept aside in remarkably little time the defenses of orthodoxy on the intellectual plane (if not yet on the planes of institutions and practical action).

For what Stalinist orthodoxy has lacked – nay, deliberately suppressed for decades except in a kind of underground of economic thought – is precisely the logic of choice, and particularly the apparatus of micro-economic rationality. Thus, it could not provide convincing answers to some of the most pressing questions of Stalinist planning itself, which is of course micro-economic planning with a vengeance. How automatic should this factory be? Should one use copper or aluminium for transmission cable? What is the best use for this piece of land? What should we export? Decisions, naturally, one way or another; but answers, no! One need not pretend that modern economics, with all its mathematical equipment and up-to-date computers, can give precise, unequivocal answers to such (and many other) questions in order to appreciate its analytic power and instrumental promise compared to the turgid dogmas of the Stalinist orthodoxy.

But there may be more to it. First, the winds of rationality may spread to other social disciplines, and they already have to some extent, as in the case of Soviet sociology. Second, modern economics lends little support to the notion of basic identity of all interests in society with one another and with the over-all social interest, a fiction on which much of Stalinist theorizing was built. The consequent re-thinking of the essential nature of a socialist society may be far-reaching. Third, as the author stresses – and this links up with our previous point as well – mathematical economics shows the way to a workable and more efficient decentralization of the economic system, with all that it implies socially and politically. Lastly, replacement of dogma by the logic of choice puts in question not only the means of action but its purposes as well. Rational decision-making is impossible without a specification of goals: small objectives to begin with, perhaps, but the larger and higher ends eventually as well. The question that the great humanist, R. H. Tawney, once flung at capitalism – To What End Do The Wheels Turn? – has now, in effect, been flung by the super-technicians of Soviet mathematical economics at *their* social order. Of course, no on-going social order can really answer this question, least of all the ultra-conservative Soviet one of today – which is surely a major reason why the high ambitions of Soviet mathematical economists will continue to be frustrated insofar as one can see ahead.

In a word, the extreme fortunes of Soviet mathematical economics – as both thought and practice – in the past were politically determined, and its future also rests in the political balance. At the end of the 'twenties Stalin suppressed mathematical economics (and many of its most eminent scholars) for political reasons that are too well known to be stated here. It and the few scholars that survived the quarter century of terror were rehabilitated after the Twentieth ('Anti-Stalin') Party Congress of 1956, thanks to Khrushchev's political 'thaw' and the promise of economic efficiency inherent in mathematical economics. But the political re-freeze of the 'sixties, especially after Khrushchev's fall, brought new limits to the freedom of expression in the social sciences. Mathematical economics may have suffered less than the other social sciences from this reaction, owing to its technical and instrumental nature. It may even benefit from the divisions in the present collective leadership. Yet its political bounds are quite clearly drawn: anything that threatens the power of the leadership, the Party *apparat,* and the entrenched bureaucracies, which includes everything that would significantly liberalize the existing economic institutions, is unwelcome and often simply censored out. The fact of the mathematization of Soviet economics – as the author concludes, referring to a Soviet authority – may indeed be an irreversible process, and thereby also – as the author more cautiously adds – an indication of its internationalization. But we still have to wish Soviet economics well in regard to freedom of intellectual inquiry and latitude of practical application.

viii

Contents

Preface

The gestation of this book goes back to the latter 1960s when the Royal Institute of International Affairs (Chatham House) offered me its auspices for an inquiry into the dramatic change in Soviet economic *thinking* resulting from the assimilation of the mathematical approach, methods and techniques.

The process (which at the time of the offer was gaining its momentum) must be of interest to the Western mathematically oriented economist, if only because of the traditional, truly exceptional brilliance of the Russian-Soviet mathematicians, pre-eminent, or at least unsurpassed, in some of the most important fields. This interest is too obvious and legitimate to need justification. But, we submit, the change has certain characteristics and elements which should merit the attention of a wider class of reader beyond that circle of specialists.

To begin with, quite a few economists outside this circle may wish to gain an idea of the 'conversion' of Soviet economic doctrine, specifically planning doctrine, to formalized methodology, which it repudiated for decades as a matter of principle. To be introduced – if only very broadly – to the substance, background, causes, and progress of the process in Soviet economics, specifically economics of macro-planning, may be attractive to Western economists in general who, more often than not, have but little chance of keeping *au courant* with happenings in that area. Certain contemporary tendencies in Western macro-economic theory, specifically in normative macro-economics, and more specifically in the growingly 'respectable' theory of economic planning, could be expected to enhance this interest.

The wave-like impact of the process under discussion here, its scale and intensity, its results – disappointments and successes, actual and potential – make acquaintance with it helpful to any student of Soviet economics and economic theory; and the knowledge of certain aspects of it necessary to a student of Soviet developments in general. More, some of these aspects could possibly interest a still wider group of observers of the international stage, and they do so on various counts – some very general, some more particular. Thus the Soviet case history of experience in mathematics of system optimization with a view to 'marrying' it with modern computational technology may be found by some students fascinating in its own right. (Richard Bellman, in one of his many wonderful *obiter dicta,* remarks that one of the most profound concepts in current culture is that of a system; and that the ramifications of this product of civilization will occupy the intellectual world for a long time to come.[1] Soviet efforts – at least in a sense – come

[1] R. Bellman, *Introduction to mathematical theory of controlled processes* (London, 1967), vol. 1.

under this heading.) The particular circumstances may be of interest to other students. For here we are concerned with what, as far as this writer knows, is the unique environment where a virtual ban on mathematical reasoning in an important domain of intellectual pursuit (as well as in application of mathematical tools in planning and running the economy) was in force for a quarter of a century,[2] to be lifted finally as part and parcel of a search for ways of reforming the obsolescing economic mechanism and, what is now understood as closely interrelated, for ways of modernizing the supporting economic thought – at the time when traditional Soviet economic theorizing suffered from acute sterility. Furthermore, as will appear almost at every step of our discussion, the process observed has brought about an intensive East-West intellectual traffic of ideas where in the pre-mathematical phase all lines of communication were effectively blocked: an intellectual East-West bridge in an important domain has thus been constructed. (It is my good fortune that these important 'side-aspects' were perceived by Andrew Shonfield, the distinguished economist then Director of Studies, now the Director of the Royal Institute of International Affairs, at a time when the reasons why my topic should come within the province of the Chatham House sponsorship were less evident than they are today.)

However, as my work progressed, catering to the different angles of interest of the two groups of potential readers revealed serious limitations. On the one hand, to do justice to the subject in a way which would merit the interest of the mathematically oriented scholar, the presentation of, and working with, the mathematical apparatus was an obvious necessity. Restraining oneself in this would severely affect whatever value our study could have for the specialist scholar. On the other hand, to the potential 'non-mathematical' reader who could be expected to be interested in the specific aspects of the story, the mathematical apparatus of the work would inevitably be a cause of unwieldiness and a handicap. In a word, handling both 'versions' between the same two covers – the formal and the informal version – carried the risk of falling between two stools. This was the motive which induced Chatham House at some stage to suggest breaking up the study and devoting a separate book to the non-mathematical handling of the matter, self-contained and sufficiently concise. (By that time the work had grown to about a quarter of a million words, far in excess of the projected size; I appreciate Chatham House's considerate treatment of my dilemma on this point.)

This, then, is how the present version in exclusively non-formal

[2] Note that almost half a century ago – in the mid 1920s – a Soviet economist, V. A. Bazarov, made the remarkable point that while the optimum determining of the economy's perspective developments is beyond the capabilities of Soviet planning, some of its simpler problems were solvable already at that time by means of modern mathematics! He added that in the meantime the Soviet planner had to content himself with crude approximations. (Cf. *Plan. khoz.*, no. 7, 1926.)

language came into being. I should perhaps add that because of its character it was thought advisable here to offer to the reader a historical background: to include in it a brief survey of the main turning points in Soviet economic thinking for the past half century, and to point out the peaks of interest with which the whole study deals.

Naturally, isolating our two 'versions' of the story creates its own problems. With respect to one we may note, however, that both volumes – this, and the other addressed essentially to the mathematical specialist (entitled *Mathematical Theory in Soviet Planning*) are expected to appear almost simultaneously. Thus a reader who may wish to acquaint himself with certain more strictly theoretical discussions, and specifically with some more rigorous formulations of certain problems relating to chief topics, is invited to look at the second volume.

Finally a few words of acknowledgement of my debt of gratitude. To the Director of the Royal Institute of International Affairs – my debt for initiating the study and giving throughout his friendly support; it is too obvious from what I said at the outset that any further expression is unnecessary. In most other cases I can do no better than restate in brief my words of appreciation from the 'twin' volume. I am indebted to the successive Directors of Studies, James Fawcett and Ian Smart: to Ian Smart for his untiring efforts to ensure the appearance of the book. My warm appreciation goes to Miss Hermia Oliver for offering to this study her unique editorial expertise and for editorially disciplining me. The dedication to my wife is only a token of my recognition of her devoted support and help.

It is a pleasure to express appreciation of fruitful conversations over the years – on many a subject of this study – with my colleague at the LSE, Peter Wiles.

I wish also to express my warmest thanks to Gregory Grossman for so kindly providing a foreword to this study.

A. Z.

London School of Economics
March 1974

The revolution; substance and background

(1) The very title of our book contains the opinion that Soviet economics has undergone a change which in its intensity could and should be classified as revolutionary. This revolution is, in our submission, due to the assimilation, over the past decade and a half, of mathematical methods and techniques. To anticipate our argument, while the process has thus occurred essentially on the methodological and technical plane, it has had a profound impact on the very mode of economic thinking. At least a cursory historical outline may be helpful in justifying this opinion.

Until the Bolshevik revolution Russian economics was developing within the main stream of Western thought – with some discernible Marxian inclination since the turn of the nineteenth century. From our angle, of particular interest may be the work of Dmitriev around the year 1900, who at that time identified himself with a good deal of what he found in Cournot and Walras as well as Ricardo,[1] and who was also a precursor of some techniques in mathematical analysis.

The Bolshevik political triumph gave to the Marxian doctrine a dominant, and before long a recognized, monopolistic position. Very broadly, this amounted first and foremost to providing a basis for the critique and repudiation of the whole of post-Ricardian non-Marxist body of economics. As time passed the officially adhered to economic doctrine tended increasingly to be confined to not much more than more or less literal restatement and exegesis of the Marxian texts – with a strong *ne varietur* rule.

Owing to the very well-known Marxian classics' restraint (evolved as a reaction against utopian socialist predecessors) in committing themselves with respect to the economics of the future socialist society, such a state of affairs amounted to a theoretical vacuum. It seems to us justifiable to think, however, that during the phase of the breakthrough to, and 'spiral-wise' acceleration of, planned growth, Soviet thinking – of empiricist character *par excellence* – was adjusting itself to the needs of actual practice. This does not mean that certain broad ideas derived from Marx, which were congenial to this thinking, were not used as its theoretical validation. This is true in particular in respect of economic strategy; but, as we will try to show, not exclusively of strategy.

Examples may be given for our proposition in looking to Marx for support of empirically built up principles. One of them is indeed of outstanding importance. During the critical phase of industrial advance, Marx's law on the 'first department' outpacing the second was invoked as a justification of the strategic precept for growth propulsion (in the Marxian conceptual framework, the terms first and second department stand respectively for sectors producing producer goods and consumer goods). It is in fact in our view tenable that Marx's model of growth – the first to be formulated with any degree of rigour in the history of economics – well articulated the Soviet stand, oriented as it was towards as fast as possible 'catching up and overtaking' the industrialized capitalist economies. (The merits of the Marxian growth model find a good deal of new recognition – as witnessed by M. Morishima's *Theory of Economic Growth*, 1969,[2] and subsequent work. The crucial point, however, is that with the change of the environment – and consequently of strategy – the Soviet economist has become aware of the underlying assumptions of the model, and of the limitations of the strategy precept derivable from it, for practicable purposes.)

Another example concerns the economic mechanism. One of the few – if only very broad – ideas offered by the Marxian classics to the architects of the socialist economy was that it could and should dispense with money: the planned socialist money-free system would correspond to the extinction – under socialism – of the law of value on Marx's definition. Except for the short period of the civil war, when money-based economy virtually disintegrated, this Marxian conception was repudiated by official Soviet doctrine (or rather, which for all practical intents and purposes amounts to the same thing, it was relegated to the future millennial scarcity-free phase of communism). Another example brings us still closer to our immediate theme: while dissociating itself from the concept of a non-monetary economic mechanism, Soviet theory on the mechanism of central planning crystallized as one resting on quantity-term (physical-term) calculation. Again the stand of Soviet economic doctrine, or perhaps in this case one would say Soviet planning doctrine, has evolved from a realistic appraisal of the possibilities – related to the limited technical potentialities of that time – of a price-termed calculus as an instrument. And again – typically for the eclecticism in accepting Marxian ideas for the economics of socialism – Marx has on this point been invoked for corroboration of what was found feasible and useful on practical grounds, given the existing techniques. Parenthetically we may only remark that this would seem to suggest that – as far as economics applied in real life goes – the Soviet attitude, far from having the doctrinaire character so often ascribed to it, has been to a remarkable degree pragmatic.

Time and again we have alluded to the build-up of a set of principles in support of a practicable approximation to what has been adopted as a desideratum – in the grand policy of economic development and the institutional-operational framework. Both are in fact intimately related. A few observations have already been made on the first; we shall now make a few more on the second.

Design of the traditional mechanism: outlived rationale and obsolescence

(2) It has been accepted from the very beginning of its Soviet history that socialism implies: (a) the effective control of the economy by society, organized in the socialist state, in pursuance of its objectives (implying in particular the full control of productive resources by means

of appropriate institutions), and (b) a planned steering by the state of the course of economic life – as a postulate of rationality with respect to point (a) and made possible by the nature of the socialist society. In fact point (a) has been derived from the axiomatically accepted philosophy which accords to the state, as the embodiment of the society, the supremacy of the intra-temporal, and still more of the inter-temporal, system of preferences (see below, section 12). Point (b) has been argued also in terms of efficiency in the use of scarce resources and continuous, undisturbed advance; the elimination of cycles caused by supply-demand disequilibria would be one of the main gains.

It is from the combination of the two principles that the Soviet approach to planning has been evolved. This approach in the accepted terminology is known as 'democratic centralism'. In very broad outline it means this. The plan is conceived as the expression of the centre's goals in regulating the economic life of the country. Without this being necessarily articulated, the accepted premise is that tools of indirect regulation, of indirect guidance towards these objectives, are not dependable. This would apply to all the instruments familiar from the theory and practice of capitalism – money and credit, fiscal and tariff policies, and so on; it would apply first of all, with important implications, to the potentially chief instrument, i.e. the price in its widest sense, that is including rate of interest. Hence the reliance – again we would think primarily as a matter of practicability rather than of principle – on direct guidance; in other words, on as detailed as practically possible direct command, in non-price terms, from the central controlling authority to the executive echelon, however institutionalized.

We have said that in rejecting the Marxian precepts Soviet doctrine has retained the price tool; but (as against a fair number of students who see in it only a face-saving formula) we accept the Soviet tenet that the nature of price under socialism *is* different from that under capitalism; that at least conceptually in the Soviet system, price and price-termed tools are reduced to an auxiliary, essentially accounting function (auxiliary that is in relation to the quantity-termed command; this relates to the fact that money performs essentially an accounting function; it is *neither* a means of exchange nor a store of value); hence it is a facet of this system – again at least conceptually – in that price is not functioning as the basic signal in the economy's information mechanism and/or as a parameter of decision-making. We have placed the emphasis on the conceptual stand; we may in fact extend it to the lack of any consistent articulation which commits Soviet planning theory to the principle. Indeed, our dichotomy (physical-term v. money-term planning and steering the economy) has had hardly any systematic and explicit presentation in Soviet traditional doctrine. Still less has it had any 'pure' and consistent reflection in practice. Quite possibly such consistency could not be obtained in practice – if only because of the astronomical amount of detail with which real life confronts the centre entrusted with the task of complete control (and the technical aspects of aggregation and disaggregation, on which we will not enlarge at this stage, crucial though they are). The inconsistencies being inevitably a cause of error and disturbance, they quite probably did not exceed a tolerable weight (tolerable given the advantages the system secured – judging from the adopted stand). They did not, that is, decisively affect the workability of the mechanism – certainly not up to a certain stage in economic development. To put this very roughly, the character of the environment – its underdevelopment – was simplifying over a long period the processes of information, choice-making, and control; and in turn the nature of the planning regime – and the type of strategy adopted – were enhancing the simplification. The strategy choices could be confined to a narrow range of processes and products – fuels, metals, basic machinery, essentials for human consumption; and the planning regime would support this. In particular, the simplifications indicated have been of importance in handling the element which is otherwise extremely difficult to cope with in planning, the time factor. For reasons stated, the horizon in plan construction would be such as to make it almost timeless. To anticipate a theoretically more expanded argument, the celebrated von Neumann system,[3] abstract as it is owing to the strength of the underlying assumptions which move it away from reality, may be considered as the formalization of the traditional Soviet strategy. This is so because it models a monotonic expansion of the system – with time horizon reaching out into infinity – with a single growth-propelling sector; this sector's maximized output is man-hours and its minimized input the means of subsistence. It is indeed agreed by most students that the model, in its classical form, fits an economy which is not 'welfare-constrained'[4] and this holds for the Soviet economy over the critical phase of growth.[5]

While rational, given the objective circumstances and the adopted desiderata, the system has been inescapably subject to diminishing returns; it has begun to show at some moment symptoms of declining efficiency. On the diagnosis of this phenomenon, there has been remarkable agreement among Soviet and outside students. The principal causes are found in the growing and interrelated degree of complexity of the economic, social, and political environment and strategy. The complexity has been demonstrably rising with advancing maturity (this among other things entails an almost exponentially increasing amount of detail to be controlled, with correspondingly growing difficulties of aggregation). The corollary has been the shift from the strategy of acceleration to that of stability in growth – with the corresponding reflex on the time-horizon in planning. The type of growth has been undergoing a qualitative as well as a quantitative change – at least in the economic strategist's intention: a shift from the traditional extensive, to the more exacting – from the planner's point of view – intensive type of growth. (The problem involves – as E. A. G. Robinson

4

rightly pointed out – the philosophy of techniques.[6] As a matter of fact Soviet literature has been indicating the economy's resistance to such a shift.) To sum up in one sentence: the growing sophistication of the economy has been invalidating the simplifying assumptions of the methodology of planning and running the Soviet economy, causing their obsolescence, and making the need for more refined techniques and tools increasingly acute.

Computational explosion; impact on search for modernized mechanism

(3) By a historical accident these developments have coincided with a remarkable advance in methods of rigorous formulation and quantification of economic plans (the word 'accident' need not be taken literally; a certain degree of causal relation between the phenomena mentioned may be discoverable, but we will not enlarge on this). The advances we have in mind are, first, the mathematization of economic thinking – what is of obvious importance in Soviet conditions, the mathematization of planning theory – and, second, electronic computation. The fabulous pace in the development of the latter has clearly acted as a powerful stimulant in the progress in the former. No doubt it has helped to overcome the reservations Soviet doctrine has had with respect to mathematics in economics. By the same token, it is arguable that prior to the 'explosion' of 'automized' computation, formalized planning methodology would be of limited, if any, practical utility. Only the combination of both has opened up new vistas for the theory and practice of planning. And this has shaped the Soviet standpoint. To quote, as representative of the new attitude and aspirations, Academician Fedorenko's words:

The doctrine of planning and controlling the economy should become an exact science in the full sense of the word; a highly effective instrument for the creation and development of an integrated system of optimal planning and controlling the country's economy on the basis of expanded application of economic-mathematical methods and computation techniques.

It is a tenet of Fedorenko and his associates that one of the aspects – one of the most important aspects – of the 'contemporary scientific-technological revolution' is 'a scientific-technological revolution in the domain of controlling social production' based on 'contemporary advances in economic sciences, mathematics . . . and wide application of computational and informational techniques . . .'.[7,8]

What we are saying now may provide perhaps at least an understandable clue to the virtual ban on mathematical argument and methodology in Soviet planning doctrine for well over the post-1930 quarter of a century. The reason usually advanced – that the historical link between mathematical methods and the economics of capitalism had created an idiosyncratic attitude – is hardly satisfying intellectually in the 1970s. (Incidentally, the publication of Marx's exercises in mathematical economics, whatever their intrinsic value, has disposed of the argument.)[9]

Another clue in the search for rational explanation of the anti-mathematical bias might be perhaps detected in the link between mathematical argument at the critical time of the 'breakthrough phase' of the Soviet economy and the adopted strategy. Elsewhere I have conjectured that the otherwise inexplicable condemnation to oblivion of Feldman's brilliant construct[10] – presenting to the economic strategist the choice between balanced and unbalanced growth, with the implications and consequences – might perhaps explain the official standpoint: for by indicating choice, it conflicted with the official tenet of there being no viable strategy for rapid growth other than the one pursued – the strategy of unbalanced growth – on a suitable definition. (It is to be noted that now that mathematical reasoning is admitted – and the choice of strategies for development is not questioned – the work of Feldman is being rescued from oblivion, and the claim is being made on his behalf to chronological priority in the strict formulation of the Domar–Harrod type of growth processes.)[11]

Mathematical techniques in Soviet economics; historical note

(4) The first area of reception of mathematical techniques[12] in Soviet planning doctrine has been that of inter-industry analysis. The early 1920s saw Soviet pioneering in statistical 'balances of the national economy' reflecting intersectoral flows. It is these attempts – intended to be a help in an ex-ante elaboration of the plan, in fact serving as the ex-post presentation of the performance and its analysis – little formalized though they were and not offering any efficient mathematical devices, that provoked the verdict of incompatibility with Marxian doctrine; and also, significantly, of resting on the concept of equilibrium and thereby being in opposition to the strategy of growth.

The attempts were abandoned – to be resumed only decades later. In the meantime Soviet planning practice largely expanded the use of the 'material balance' – a simple statement of requirements and ways of meeting them. (Starting from some basic commodities, the range of such 'balances' has been gradually extended to embrace the labour force, investment, foreign trade, and so on.) Extremely crude as the instrument is, it has become the most important tool, indeed the mainstay of Soviet planning techniques. The 'balances' are essentially built up in quantity (physical) terms; for some categories of goods (such as complicated engineering products and more so for investment) money terms had to be adopted (remember our point about inconsistency in this matter). In any case the link of the system of balances with that of national accounts is tenuous.

Method of balances and progress towards Leontievian ideas

(5) The 'method of balances' (so it is termed in traditional planning doctrine) is related in Soviet practice with that termed 'material-technical supply'. What this means and entails in practice has been described by the late Academician Nemchinov, one of the main promoters of the mathematization of planning. To quote him:[13]

[under the system of] ... material-technical supplies we still operate a *sui generis* rationing system ... The top-heavy procedure of ex-ante applications, followed by repeated revisions of allocations before the final completion and implementation ... results in an inevitable malaise of our economy.

By the time Soviet planning returned to inter-industry analysis it was able to claim a tremendous advance, thanks to the Leontief-designed apparatus. It is this apparatus that has secured rigour and powerful workability and versatility to the overall balance. Indeed it was *the* opening step in the revolution in planning which is our theme.

Here – very broadly – we have in mind the following aspects.

1. While inevitably conventionalized, the equations embraced by the mathematical input-output formulation of the plan do present perfect consistency. Nothing even remotely comparable on this count can be expected from the traditional Soviet method. Under this, as indicated in what has been said before, each 'material balance' – budgeting the proposed uses and availabilities of an item – is self-contained; there is no explicit link with and practicable check on other items; indeed, no means for an overall balancing of the economy is provided. (To return to the point made, as against the set of material balances, the input–output system does correspond to the no longer shunned general-equilibrium approach.)

2. One of the most powerful techniques provided by the Leontief methodology is that for computation of full order, that is direct and indirect inputs – 'all along the line' (or 'from the beginning of history') – per unit of a given kind of output. This is carried out technically by means of matrix 'inversion'. Various methods of inverting the matrix – exact and approximate – are known in practice, the choice from among these is made on several considerations (precision, handiness, and so on). While the traditional Soviet method has to content itself with the – poorly reflected – direct relationships in the economy, the Leontief method has offered a new, wide, and deep insight into the economy's system of 'linkages'. Its significance for planning from this angle can hardly be overestimated.

3. It is the structural feature of the input–output system that provides the 'photograph' of the formation of the product – in all-economy planning, of the national product. It can be built up in physical terms and/or price terms. It is the latter kind of the all-economy numerical image of the economy that is of particular interest. It shows – along the rows – how the output of each sector is used up for an in-

termediate product, supporting further production and/or final uses; and – down the columns – how it is formed by itself with (intermediate) contributions from other sectors and prime-factor contributions. The latter can be summarized as composed of wage-type and other rewards to non-labour factors, including entrepreneurship.

4. From what has been said there follow very important indications for pricing. The method shows how the price of a product is reduced to a sum-total of prime factor and intermediate contribution cost – all corresponding to the consistency of the system. Constructionally, this quantifies the (averaged) cost-plus-price which has been theoretically adopted by the traditional techniques. (To avoid misunderstanding – and because of the importance of the matter – we may already introduce a caveat here; while the price structure thus arrived at reflects its fundamental logic and corresponds to consistency, it does not necessarily correspond to efficiency. Nor does it *per se* reflect the impact of time. More on this later.)

Here we may once again touch upon the issue of physical versus price-term planning. The basic idea that has inspired those responsible for the revolution in Soviet planning economics has been expressed in these terms by Academician Nemchinov:[14]

... the process of production and exchange can proceed without bottlenecks only where a system of simultaneous equations underlies the national-economic plan equations, where the economic valuation and plan prices are mutually coordinated and correspond to the physical volume-term structure of output and consumption.[15] Under the conditions of a capitalist economy – a market economy – this is an elemental process: with us it should be a plan-wise controlled and conscious process with the commodity exchange suitably organized.

5. The powerful Leontief apparatus had permitted a radical change in the focus of national economic planning. This change can in fact be well related to the change in the economic environment (indeed going beyond this, to the change in the social-political environment, a subject which is however not covered by our study).

In the traditional method the Soviet planner has always been working from the intermediate inputs towards the final bill of goods. It is in fact the intermediate rather than the ultimate products – i.e. iron, steel, building materials, fuels, basic chemicals – that have been focal in plan construction, the idea being that until some sufficiently high level in the production of these commodities is achieved or attained, the Soviet economic strategist cannot have freedom of manoeuvre in setting his targets for the 'final' products. Thus the approach can be convincingly related to the specific requirements of the breakthrough phase, the phase of 'horizonless' self-accelerating growth – in autarkic conditions (the political as well as economic premises of the autarky will not be discussed here). The production thus oriented is in fact helping to build up what was thought of as the industrial basis – the stock of productive capacities, in turn related to the strategic principle of priority for capital goods (see above). In this strategy consumption is the residuum, in a sense a component of the *cost* of growth and as such, logically, to be minimized – on this one may refer to the logic of the von Neumann model hinted at before (p. 4).

This traditional approach has gradually tended to outlive its rationale – as the economy has approached maturity, with the corresponding gradual change in social attitudes as well. In the process the focus is being shifted towards the composition of the final bill of goods. And the newly assimilated apparatus of the mathematized inter-industry analysis, plus (this must be borne in mind all the time) the technological progress in computation have made it possible for the planner to reverse his point of departure in plan construction; to start, that is, from the desirable 'final bill' and to work his way towards the overall production plan – patently something more in agreement with the nature of an 'intensified' economy.

Jump from 'five fingers plus abacus' into the electronic era

(6) Having said this much on the immense advantages of the mathematization of planning *à la* Leontief – advantages permitting a jump from the era of 'five-finger-plus-abacus' computation to that of the modern world of electronics – we may now, to balance the picture, say something about its limitations.

First and foremost, there is the difficulty of the sheer size of the plan problem. The list of commodities – the so-called 'nomenclature' – of the Soviet economy contains around 15 million items. Whatever the reasonably expected advances in formalized planning methodology and computation in the foreseeable future, there is no possibility of directly handling any substantial part of this. Whether the set directly entering the central national economic plan reaches as many as 1,000 items (as it actually does under the primitive and imprecise traditional method) or only around 500-600 (as seems to be the fact under the mathematical system), the number in any case can only represent a small fraction of one *pro mille* of the total! If the embodying of the total 'nomenclature' of commodities is included in the postulate of the plan's consistency, then consistency is in any case clearly just a will-o'-the-wisp. Criticism of the formalized method on this count is misdirected: if at all, it would be – and meaningfully – directed at planning as such.

The problem we are discussing here is a part of what Bellman has described as the 'curse of dimensions'. (Trotsky, who when at the centre of power was identified with faith in all-embracing planning, perceived the implications of this 'curse' when in exile. In an oft-quoted passage of an essay published in 1932 he wrote:

If there existed the universal mind – that projected itself into the scientific fancy of Laplace; a mind that could register simultaneously all the processes of nature and of society; that could measure the dynamics of their motion, that could forecast the results of their interactions, such a mind, of course, could *a priori* draw up a faultless and exhaustive economic plan, beginning with the number of hectares of wheat and come down to the last button for a vest.[16]

It may be fascinating to speculate whether and how Trotsky would have qualified these second thoughts of his had he survived to witness the computational revolution. But it is legitimate to say that the Laplacean dilemma which he pointed out has not been exorcized from Central Planning Offices.)

(The problem of the plan's size not being specific to any particular type of planning techniques – thus not specific to the new, formalized, as against the traditional, non-rigorous methods either – calls for some adequate way of bringing groups of commodities under one heading. In this way, as Peter Wiles has argued, aggregative commodities are 'created': this is being done with reference to some relevant properties – relevant in particular from the economic as distinct from the technological point of view.) At best one can only expect that mathematical-economic ingenuity would make it tolerably workable. As a matter of fact, the pace at which the handicap of the Bellmanian 'curse of dimensions' is being overcome may justify a certain dose of optimism.

A related point. Prognostication apart, what has been said here may give an idea as to how exacting are the requirements with respect to the technological 'scaffolding' (for a 'perspective' plan) of the input-output structure. Again the mathematization of planning has only revealed them; certainly it has not created them, although in the rigorous framework the trouble is accentuated (see section 23). (It has given a spur to considerable Soviet effort to give increasing precision to this framework: effort to get reliable parameters such as those of capital-intensity of production, 'norms' of capital-construction periods, indexes of branch-patterning of production, and so on.) The accentuated trouble is to a great extent that of the lack of sufficient information at the planning centre – yet another stumbling-block to which we have to return at every point of this story (see section 17).

Now it is true that experience with the input–output technique has proved that it is only a surprisingly small proportion – something like one-tenth – of the contents of the technological matrix of the plan that is decisive for results. But even for this amount the supply of data is not adequate. It is with respect to the input–output technique, the one which, among the mathematical techniques, has been by now most effectively assimilated, that the issue of the hopelessly unadjusted system of channelling and processing the information flows has come to the fore.

The following is the schema of computation of the input–output (inter-industry) balance with and iterative calculation of investment:

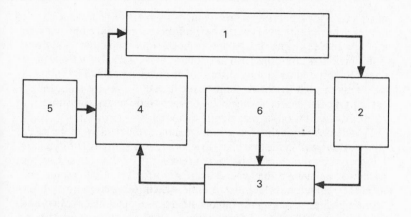

1. Macro-economic model (computation of the volume and component structure of national income).
2. Computation of the level and structure (components, branches) of final product.
3. Computation of gross output.
4. Computation of requirements in investment; confrontation with resources.
5, 6. Respective capital and input – output coefficients.

Source: A. N. Yefimov, ed., *Mezhotraslevoy balans i proportsii narodnogo khozyaistva* (1969).

Formalized techniques for consistency of plans

(7) Some of the limitations of the technique stem from the inherent characteristics of its design.

Firstly, the original input–output construct is linear (all inter-industry relationships are taken to be expressible by algebraic equations of the first degree in their variables). Patently this fails exactly to reflect economic realities: the reflection of economies and diseconomies of scale is the principal case in point. We shall have an opportunity to say something about the efforts to overcome this obstacle.

Secondly, the relationships between phenomena observed are taken to be unique and constant. The technology adopted is assumed to be the only workable one. There again this is patently a restrictive assumption – restrictive with respect to what we know in reality. Various ways have been elaborated to weaken the assumption of technological rigidity.

Thirdly, the construct is essentially static: in other words it gives an 'instantaneous' portrait of economic life – at a fixed point in time. This characteristic is no handicap when we employ the input–output technique for ex-post analytical purposes, but planning by its very nature is oriented towards the future it tries to cope with. This is a very major shortcoming which calls for more comment.

A number of methods have been devised for relaxing this limitation too, and some of them have been tested in planning practice. The simplest one which suggests itself is to build up a statistical input–output 'picture' for the terminal time-point of the plan, due allowance being made for the requirements of the beyond-the-horizon development, and then, on one principle or another, to break up the 'picture' – starting from the initial up to the terminal point – into a series of intermediate ones, corresponding to the institutional arrangements. The inherent weakness of such simple methods is the lack of intrinsic ('endogenous' in the particular sense) linkage between such 'sub-images' over time: the lack of dynamics, on its meaningful definition.

What can be thought of as a fundamental dynamization of the static construct is owed in the first place to its originator himself. The dynamic Leontief construct – or to be more precise, the methods based on the particular as against the general solution of the set of differential and difference equations which express the system of interrelations in the economy – has been experimented with in Soviet planning practice, and the complex mathematical algorithmization has proved not easy to handle. The difficulties were related by Academician Fedorenko largely to the confluence of those entailed in the matrix of capital coefficients and those due to the requirement of constant direct input–output ratios. (The theoretical problems involved in the dynamization of the input–output system have been discussed by the author elsewhere.)[17]

Parallel with the theoretical explorations, intensive empirical work has gone on, for quite a time, with a view to injecting the input–output system with some 'dose' of dynamism; whatever their theoretical virtues, some of these efforts have helped to expand the practising planner's mathematical equipment. The way such a 'dose of dynamics' has been injected into the design for the Soviet plan for the second half of the 1960s may give an idea of the progress made in organically tying up production and investment. The structure of national income and the assumed level of efficiency of newly formed capital stock were the starting point. From this the broad figures of national product and investment in the terminal plan year were derived; then year-by-year figures were obtained through interpolation: three to four iterations were found sufficient to harmonize the yearly volumes and structures of national product and investments. Clearly this had to be supplemented by some method of dealing with the post-plan developments inasmuch as they affect the economy in the plan period. Here the starting point is the appraisal, in a more or less traditional fashion, of the need for the build-up of new capacities for this development; and this is being done by two methods. By one of them the model is elaborated for an additional four or five years with an approximate calculation of incremental capacities based on the accepted standards – 'norms' – for uncompleted construction; the other simply accepts the hypothesis of continuing statistical trends.

By now the Gosplan claims to have elaborated and made operational some more advanced models, formed of a linear-equations system, correlating manpower, investment, and production with marginal (rather than overall) capital-output coefficients and investment output lags to ensure that the year's planned growth of capacities is sufficient to achieve the incremental outputs in the coming year or years. This technique is now believed to be reliable for a stage-by-stage construction of the multi-period plan, and manageable if only for a strategy-determining, small-dimension (around 30 sectors) exercise. A larger-scale model (over 120 sectors) – linear with constant coefficients – is apparently in use for an iterative evaluation of needs in investment.

With these kinds of instruments the planning procedure as outlined by a team of the Gosplan's Research Institute would be as follows. One starts with a dynamic model for calculating the inter-industry balance of relatively small dimensions, say between twenty and thirty items, in money terms.[18] This helps to select the variants of the overall 'hypothesis of development' (taking into account the broad development potentialities of the economy's leading branches); to select realistic variants of levels and structure of national income and product as supported by resources – materials, labour, and finance – under the postulated efficiency. On parallel lines sectoral 'hypotheses' are elaborated embracing output volumes and structures, requirements in resources, exports, and imports, account being taken of expected direction and level of technical progress. On this basis the primary information for the expanded inter-industry balance, in quantities and prices, is evolved: also indices of the final bill of goods, related to a system of technological coefficients – coefficients of fixed capital, circulating capital, and labour. The next step is the calculation of variants, in quantities and prices.

Physical and money-term planning; aggregation problem

(8) We may note here that integration of accounts in physical and money terms – now a subject of intensive discussion in Soviet mathematical-planning literature – comes up against some very serious hurdles.[19] The lack of such an integration has always been a very major handicap of Soviet planning. For reasons which go beyond our theme, Soviet planning has been intrinsically of the non-money-term kind. And it is interesting that in this respect the mathematization of Soviet planning has not so far brought about a radical change, much as it has the support of the mathematical school. In fact, when on the initiative of one of the principal promoters of mathematization, Nemchinov, the effect of implanting the matrix calculus in the firm's plan information – as a basis of the national-economic system of information – was investigated, all the emphasis was on the physical-terms facet. And, it appears, the money-term information still remains largely unexploited. The problem faced now is how to carry out the link-up of the matrix-calculation of the lower echelon with the overall block-matrix of the system of macro-economic information. It would seem, in the light of reports from the USSR Academy's Central Mathematical-Economic

Institute (TsEMI), that the vertical integration of the information, its basis being what it is, comes up at that echelon against technical difficulties. (As a matter of fact this would relate, in our submission, to the lack of dependability of the money-term valuation under Soviet planning. Quite possibly it is the awareness of this factor that motivated Nemchinov's stress on the physical-term aspect of the matrix.)

However, the Gosplan scheme does postulate that the physical and money-term information is to be centralized and made use of in the selection of non-decomposable 'blocks' of the national-income matrix and thereby the clarification of its structural characteristics.

A scheme of such blocks for the purpose of planning practice has been aptly modelled by the Research Institute of the Gosplan (we reproduce the model on p. 15).[20] The first three blocks describe production and redistribution of output – for the national economy in both the sectoral and commodity profiles, in physical and money terms (on the principle of a 'pure' branch, that is a single commodity-group branch). The next three blocks depict the formation, redistribution, and use of incomes. The last three blocks show the resources in capital stock, investment, and labour force, and their distribution – in both the productive and non-productive spheres.

The guiding idea of the model is to integrate the national accounts in both physical and money (price) terms. Thus the role of the schema is to help the central planner (1) to determine the level and structure of the overall economic indices (output, national income, consumption, capital formation, and so on), (2) to build up – starting from the overall plan conception – material and money-term balances, (3) to appraise the requirements in volumes of capital and capacity formation, (4) to appraise the economy's needs in major categories of material resources, (5) to calculate basic indices for labour resources and wages (sectoral allocation in particular), (6) to determine basic indices of production cost and profitability – in sectoral profile, (7) to determine the main indices of the financial plan of the national economy: volume and structure of money incomes formed in the material-production sphere, processes of redistribution of incomes, and the use of final incomes in non-productive consumption, investment, and so on. These data are employed in the calculation (clearly with the help of electronic computers) of the viable versions of the inter-industry balance: in effect, variants of mutually harmonized indices of development of branches and sectors and the economy are obtained.

Discovered versatility of I–0 techniques

(9) It seems legitimate to say that both theory and practice still continue to reveal some unsuspected potentialities of the amazingly vigorous and versatile Leontief instrument. Yet it is with respect of the input–output method and technique that some disappointment has been voiced in Soviet writing – specifically with respect to their ability effectively to

	Industry	Final Product	State Sector
Column headings	Unit of measurement / Iron-steel / State Sector (…) / Total / Agriculture (…) / Total intermediate use	Total / of which through trade / Social / Total / Investment / Replacement / Turnover-capital movement / Commodity-stock increment / Other elements / Exports / Imports / Total	Iron-steel (…) / State farms / Cooperative sector / Industrial sector / Total
Iron and steel . . . . Other sectors of material production Turnover tax Depreciation TOTAL	I Block of intermediate use	II Block of final product	III Block of production
Population's incomes Deductions for social insurance Incomes of state and cooperative enterprises Centralized state net income Net output, TOTAL Gross output, TOTAL	IV Block of gestation and primary re-distribution of national income	V Block of final use of national income	VI Block of re-distribution of national income

Capital stock (initial)
Additions to stock (capacities)
Depletion of stock (capacities)
Capital stock (terminal)
Construction in progress
  initial
  terminal
Other investment
TOTAL investment
Employment-yearly average
	VII
	Block of distribution of productive capital stock, investment and labour resources
		VIII
		Block of distribution of non-productive capital stock, investment and labour resources
			IX
			Block of resources – capital stock, investment, labour force

Source: Klotsvog et al., EMM (1969).

15

handle relationships of a real economic system. Once again we broach the subject of effective aggregation. Such disappointment can be ascribed in the first place to some initial overestimation of possibilities and underestimation of the difficulties. We may also note that at least two distinguished Soviet students of the problem – Volkonskiy and Yershov[21] – have come forward, in defence, with the view that to blame the 'mathematics' of the inter-industry analysis for the disappointment is not fair; that indeed it is rather the lack of imagination – mathematical-economic imagination – in exploiting the structural potentialities of the input–output construct that accounts for a good deal of the disappointment. For it is a fact that practice hardly ever makes use of the textbook form of the construct, and still less does it apply the textbook operations on and with it. We may add that the diagnosis has been accompanied by some constructive suggestions to remedy matters. One of them would consist in selecting the economy's most decisive relationships, giving them the maximum possible attention, and treating all the rest with lesser precision – in a heavily aggregated form. (In the meantime Professor Leontief, clearly thinking on the same lines, has designed a method – typical of all his work in being sophisticated and yet presented with striking simplicity – for aggregating both variables and functional relationships of the plan-matrix structure. Another device would aim at reducing and rationalizing the inter-industry 'communications' links.) An algorithm designed by Yershov provides a procedure for the calculation – clearly with the help of electronic computers – of the viable versions of the inter-industry balance: in effect variants of mutually harmonized indices of development of branches, sectors, and the economy are obtained.

Inter-industry analysis, supported by the computer, has made it possible to offer the country's economic strategists about twenty variants of the plan for the second half of the 1960s (differentiated, as it appears, *inter alia* with respect to the consumption levels and working time) – certainly an enormous step forward.

The obvious next step would be to model the formalized plan in such a way as to obtain from it a direct answer to the *policy* problem. What this is all about could hardly find a better exposition than that offered by Richard Stone[22] in his discussion of the 'natural' development of the system. One starts from the proposition of such development; one matches the number of variables and relationships, but in doing this one tries to leave the system sufficiently open to preserve an area of manoeuvre; and one introduces into it at some point a precise statement of aims.

Selecting 'best' plan variant; assimilation of Kantorivich's invention

(10) Balancing the system with the precise statement of aims is the substance of mathematical programming. To the brilliant work of Kan-

torovich in the late 1930s (chronologically preceding the independently-arrived at Dantzig construct)[23] is owed the first programming construct in the Soviet Union. Not until two decades later could its significance for planning be appreciated in that country. Its theoretical formulation apart, it was originally thought of as a method of use for some micro-economic, intra-firm patterning of production. By now it has received recognition as one of the pillars of the revolution in Soviet planning methodology, logically completing the innovation owed to Leontief. In fact the linear input–output system technically forms nothing else but a particular case of the linear programming system – one where the choice-making has been performed, as it were, behind the scenes. In other words, whereas in the former system any possible choice-making has to be carried out implicitly *outside* the mathematical framework, in programming it is made *within* this framework – and explicitly: the guiding idea is to get the best of possible plans from the operation. Thus in substance programming and planning is one and the same thing: trying to secure some adopted aims, policy goals, in the best way – economically, that is, at the least expense in terms of resources; and this holds for any efficient planning, be it macro or micro. In a significant passage in his book, Kantorovich remarked that while traditional non-mathematical planning has been essentially only qualitative, the programming approach and technique have allowed it to become quantitative as well. Describing a planning technique as non-quantitative is criticism indeed; but fair in the case. (However the reader will notice some 'dialectics' in contemporary thinking on this point when we return to the matter later on.)

Once what may be labelled the Kantorovich-Dantzig ideas established themselves in Soviet planning doctrine, they benefited from the continuous and massive work based on them in both West and East. Because of their seminal impact and their importance for the development of the mathematical revolution, we will give here at least a few broad indications of Kantorovich's fundamental formalism in their application to plan-programming.

Its point of departure is setting out the feasibility conditions, in other words conditions which have to be satisfied to make the plan viable. Next the aim of the planner is introduced: conditions – environmental and policy constraints – are determined which when satisfied make the variant *the* best among all feasible variants of the plan – in pursuit of the aim, the objective function. And it is shown that for a feasible plan to be *the* best – to be optimal – it is both necessary and sufficient that a specific set of prices exists. In other words, given the best plan we can uniquely determine the corresponding price; and vice versa – given such prices we can uniquely 'discover' the best plan.

Our last paragraph makes us return to the subject broached before – the question: has the calculation been helped in decision-making by the input–output technique, and if so, in what way?; clearly effective *choice*-making belongs to the essence of the planner's task. The answer to the question will be that by its very nature it is *not* a tool for direct choices. But it offers crucial help to the planner *firstly* by clarifying for him the alternative course he can follow, secondly by technically enabling him to make his choice. What we mean by this is that the input–output exercise as such does not yield a direct indication as to which course should be adopted; but it permits getting a set of feasible alternatives, arrived at on various assumptions, and thereby helps non-formal, 'behind-the-scenes' selection from among them. Thus the first of all the alternatives would differ with respect to the assumed technology (remember that formally in an input–output system the technology to be employed is considered to be unique), and also, say, with respect to the postulated uses of the final product. As a matter of fact, when using the traditional method – and traditional techniques – the policy-maker has hardly ever had any opportunity to operate with even one strictly consistent and feasible version of the plan: whatever consistency has usually been claimed for the latter has been purely nominal. Also, as a matter of fact, many characteristics of the Soviet traditional system of planning and executing the plan tacitly assume this. One of them is the demand to exceed the targets; surely this would tend to undermine the coherence of the plan, if it were consistent? At present, thanks to the mathematical discoveries and inventions, the central planning agency is able to submit a number of variants; and at least and at last those called on to shape the policy can consciously apply to these variants whatever criterion – corresponding to their system of preferences – they wish to adopt. True, for reasons which were indicated before, so far this applies mainly to strategy alternatives. But it is safe to say that at least the experiments with plan-programming have pointed the way to effective policy-making.

New idea of rationality; performance criteria; fundamental change in price theory

(11) The truly revolutionary effect of such formalization of the plan problem concerns several elements of the traditional mode of thinking. To begin with, it challenges the established strategic approach to the plan by the postulate of explicit, rigorously stated, policy criteria; indeed, it has stimulated thinking on the nature of these criteria – a matter which has become a centre of a very intensive controversy in contemporary Soviet economics. To anticipate our further references to this controversy, let us here place on record the standpoint of the country's principal mathematical-economic workshop – the TsEMI – as expressed by its head.[24] There is, he said at a conference devoted to the subject

a unique criterion for the development of a socialist economy – on which the selection from among the possible variants of economic development could be carried out. [... It is ...] the maximum satisfaction of material and spiritual needs of the socialist society's members. The existence of such a criterion (the goal) demands comparing – measuring various goods that are usable – by the yardstick of social utility.

The constraints at each time-point are the material ones, the manpower and the natural resources and the state of scientific-technical knowledge. The task of economic theory is to instruct how they should be optimally employed. The controversy, which is still continuing, with increasing sophistication and changing emphasis, concerns every point of this proposition – the need and the very possibility of making explicit and quantifiable the criterion of the plan, as well as its uniqueness and its essence – social utility, a concept repudiated for decades by the Soviet tradition in economics.

More immediate, from the point of view of the planning practice, has been the intellectual shock imparted by the revelation of 'duality'; the revelation of pricing inherent (as it were, embedded) in the objective, constrained as that is; the dual price being the money-term measure of the contribution which the extra unit of a scarce resource, when used in the most efficient manner, makes to the achievement of goals.

For it is a revolutionary idea, for those brought up on the traditional doctrine, that the 'embedded' price emerges in the process of the build-up of the optimal plan, and at the same time provides a check on optimality and thereby helps in correcting – improving – the plan. So it is a consequential idea that it is such a price, and only such a price, that is dependable for guiding the executive echelon towards the centre's objectives. (We may, in passing, indicate here that this revelation created the favourable climate for the adoption – in the course of the economic reforms of the 1960s – of the new regime for enterprises. The sermon preached by the mathematical-economic school has been that, since the dual price measures the resource unit's contribution to the goal, and since the enterprise's business is to get such a contribution at the minimum expense, the 'rule of the game' for its manager should be: maximize your output while minimizing your cost – or, what synthesizes this precept – maximize your profit *in such prices.* Profit has been adopted as the 'indicator of success' (to use Alex Nove's felicitous phrase)[25] and also as the basis of the system of incentives – but the crucial qualification that the profit calculation should rest on the specific kind of prices has not been implemented. Why it has not will be seen later.)

We may as well stop here and say something about why the conception of the price revealed as that being the corollary of the optimum is so completely alien to the Soviet established way of thinking. As late as 1968 a representative of that way of thinking, Dyachenko,[26] attacked the innovators – the mathematical school in planning theory – by arguing that firstly, the price which is derived from the programming exercise is 'isolated from the commodity'; that *secondly,* in the case of such a price, the valuation rests on social utility: not on the quantity of labour, 'live' and 'embodied' – the latter means in Soviet-Marxian terminology intermediate input and stock of capital goods – but on the 'contribution to the satisfaction of needs'. On both counts the price thus derived is seen by the traditionalists – in Soviet economic parlance – as 'subjective' and the traditional school postulates the 'objective' price conception. In this the doctrinally accepted theory of value is invoked: indisputably on this theory all cost forming the 'objective' basis of a commodity's price is reducible to total input – we would now say full-order, direct and indirect, input of the only value-creating factor, labour. It is only right to say that current Soviet economic literature makes a considerable effort to legitimize the innovators' stand on doctrinal grounds. In their excellent study Katsenelinboygen et al.[27] would say that the very question – what is the correct foundation of price, utility, or labour contents of a good? – is incorrectly posed; that reality is dialectical (note the phrasing of the point, acceptable to the Marxian mode of reasoning) and thus the dialectics justify the optimal-programming price. Incidentally a similar dialectical argument is applied by some to validate the *marginalist* nature of the programming price in conflict with the Marxian price concept which is based on the average cost (dialectically the mechanism would be adopted before outliving its purpose; the probing into conflicts of this kind has now been described by a leading mathematical economist as being of the genre of medieval scholasticism).[28]

The battles, which must appear to a Western economist somewhat hermetic, do nevertheless reflect the depth of revolution which is our topic here. Once again, however, we will reiterate our supposition that Marxian teaching is invoked to justify attitudes which have been formed rather independently of it – under the specific conditions of Soviet planning. Thus in the present context the postulate of 'objectivism' can without great difficulty in fact be related to the mistrust of Western-type welfare economics: a mistrust which may in turn be related first to the history of Soviet economic-strategic thinking, and secondly to practicability. (The ease with which Soviet planning doctrine in the 1960s parted with the conception of the single reward-yielding factor – when this was found both desirable and practical – is yet another piece of evidence of the non-doctrinaire attitude. As noted, since the reforms of the 1960s, the Soviet box of instruments of planning and control has contained the charge on capital – corresponding to the normative yield from it; in substance it is a rate of interest as well as the normative rate of return on investment.)

We turn to the subject of practicability. By now our reader will be aware of the momentous impact of Kantorovich's invention: it is no exaggeration to say that it has opened a new era in Soviet economic thinking. The recognition of this immense cognitive merit calls above all for making its limitations clear. To begin with, the classical programming construct has been stated as a minimum (maximum) of a linear function subject to linear constraints. Indeed it is this 'linearist' simplification – its original 'sin' – that has helped to design it in a way which has had the tremendous heuristic influence. None the less the simplification does remove the construct from the true shape of real-life relationships.

How far can this be remedied? A great deal of theoretical study has been given to the subjects of noncontinuity and nonlinearity in programming. At least one class of them has been well explored – that of nonlinear convex programming (with functions which are continuous and adequately differentiable); schemas (algorithms) for handling this class in practice have been designed and have been more or less successful. Methods have been devised for handling 'integer programmes' (in particular those tackling the question 'yes or no' – '0 or 1', which are of help in some planning problems, in planning investment in particular). Some methods have been worked out over the years for some approximative solution – especially by iterative procedures. Generally speaking, however, the nonconvex nonlinear plan-programme problem is still awaiting a solution that is both manageable and realistic.

Again, Soviet experience seems to have suggested that the manageable programme construct can adequately cope with the very broad problems of strategy. With the heavy aggregation resorted to, relatively dependable indicators, including prices, are obtainable in very-long-run planning; this applies in the first place to factor prices. By contrast, experience with programming in shorter-term and more specific planning has been rather less satisfying. (One of the sources of trouble has incidentally proved to be the valuation of capacities giving rise to 'jumps' in the course of the implementation and as often as not, already in the course of the construction itself of the plan.)[29]

Note. Some of the new Soviet models of approximate optimization are striking by their imaginatively simplified design. One value-term model produced by Klotsvog, Yershov, Buzunov, Konyus, and Abdykulova[30] stands out on both counts. The idea is to focus on changes in technological, resource-use coefficients; specifically two sets of matrices of coefficients are being built up: one of those 'inherited' at the start of the plan-interval, the other of the incremental ones taken as a weighted-mean magnitude over the plan perspective. Data on the volumes and pattern of sectoral capacities' 'maturation' are harmonized with those of engineering and construction sectors which support them. For the purpose of determining the beyond-the-horizon 'endowment' with capacities, a continuation of detectable long-run trends is assumed. Personal consumption is derived from the overall postulated consumption in constant prices with the use of equations whose parameters are empirically obtained (some kinship with Stone's model);

capacities to support the required output are derived accordingly. Personal consumption is the adopted maximand. Alternative variants differ in the restrictiveness of constraints on labour supply and the shape of applicable dynamic consumption functions.

(Incidentally, an interesting characteristic of results in numerical application of the model is the strikingly strong oscillations in growth indices of economic indicators. The fluctuations tend to be particularly strong in the plan's initial years and to die out as the restructuring of the economy, in accordance with model's conditions, progresses.)

Price of time; formalizing the effect of time

(12) When we discussed the mathematical methods and tools for handling the plan's consistency – those of inter-industry analysis – we said something on the decisive importance of treating it *sub specie temporis*. The time factor is even more all-pervasive in the optimization of the plan since, as against consistency, the concern with it essentially arises in drawing it up for *the future*.

Both original designs of programme, however – that owed to Kantorovich and that to Dantzig alike – were static. It was only later that both inventors indicated the ways of making them dynamic. Kantorovich has actually presented, in a paper of joint authorship with Makarov,[31] a model of what in Soviet planning practice is usually referred to as the 'perspective plan', i.e. a long-run or a very-long-run plan.

The ideas are very broadly as follows: Break up the foreseeable future you propose to handle in your plan into a series of time-intervals. Having done this, stretch and amend the principle of the static system. Treat the technology workable in a given time-interval, which is your plan-period unit (say a year), as a separate 'ingredient'. Then production processes will be expanded – as a rule for capital formation items – over several time-units: in each the corresponding technology is to be employed. As time moves on, some more advanced technology becomes workable – which is, of course, nothing else than the formalization of technological progress. (Technically, technologies not employed as yet in respect of the given process and/or in the given time-point, appear as zero elements in the plan matrix.) Note also that as the plan programme extends into a more and more distant future, it is reasonable to expect that the number of constraints dwindles: the 'specificity' of resources which, as it were, constrain the plan, declines over time. Beyond some time-point they would be largely reduced to manpower, with lesser and lesser differentiation at that, plus natural resources (assuming closeness of the system). Parallel with this, the 'criterial' function becomes in a sense less intricate; in the very long run it dissolves itself in the volume of consumables (or we would say what is conceptually more satisfactory – in utility).

The formalization of the dual price dynamized (see p. 28), has permitted the Soviet economist to have a new look at the vexed issues of the 'price of time' and time discount in relation to the economy's pace of growth, and in this sense efficiency. We have already indicated the doctrinal hurdles in pricing capital and in this sense time. To reformulate one of the points made, the line of reasoning is this. There is a real difficulty for a socialist economic strategist in discriminating against those 'not yet born' in favour of those alive; if there is a strong welfare-theoretic school questioning the premises of the inter-generation time discount as such in a private-enterprise – by its definition egoistic – system, the more so can one question such a discount in favour of those alive in a socialistic non-egoistic society. I have restated the argument without appraising it; in particular I have not raised one point which seems to me relevant, viz. that the definitional egoism of competitive processes does necessarily entail participants' inter-generation egoism. (Technical difficulties in applying time discount in plans with a very distant horizon will be broached in my separate volume on *Mathematical Theory in Soviet Planning*.)

The matter has always been one of perplexing dilemmas in Soviet planning thought and practice. It has indeed a chequered history. At the start of the era of planning for accelerated growth, at the time of severe capital scarcity, capital was declared a 'no-price', in a curious sense a 'free' factor. (Our attempt to rationalize this rather paradoxical kind of attitude to the strategy pursued for growth will be recalled.) Before long the concept of price of capital, chased out of one door, re-entered stealthily through another – that of planning practice; the practitioner discovered that he needed some kind of yardstick for appraising the yield from desperately scarce capital when choosing one from among several investment alternatives open to him. Significantly, the practice of setting some (in fact quite arbitrary) standards survived all doctrinal repudiation. It is the doctrine that eventually capitulated to the practitioner rather than vice versa – when a quarter of a century ago Strumilin published his famous paper on the time factor in capital-investment projects,[32] establishing the conceptual basis for the practitioner's stand. The theoretical backing provided was that of the 'law' of a continuous rise – over time – of labour productivity: once again a dialectical interpretation of an established principle permitted it to be discarded. The tool for appraising the comparative worth of investment alternatives – and setting the normative minimum, the 'threshold' of efficiency – has become part and parcel of the Soviet doctrine.[33] The theoretical support for the normative rate – a sectorally-differentiated rate of return – has been very poor indeed; that is, under the assumption of prices corresponding to the 'best' plan. And no rational principle of its quantification, although patently belonging to its essence, has been evolved over the years. The crude form of the instrument has retained its sway until the advent of the mathematical school. (Whatever refinement there has been in this field is largely owed to theoretical work in

23

countries which borrowed it from the Soviet doctrine; one of them – though with qualifications – is the adoption of a single all-national 'norm' of investment efficiency. We may only note here that what was intended to be an exceptional clause in the new rules, introduced toward the end of the 1960s and the beginning of the 1970s, has turned in Soviet practice into the readmission of the sectorally differentiated 'norms' of efficiency, thus frustrating the reformers' idea.)[34]

To restate the revolutionary impact of the mathematical school in the present context. Here too it brought about a shift toward rationality and rational articulation of Soviet planning thought. We can do no more in this brief expose than allude to Kantorovich's fundamental paper which has demonstrated the interconnection of the capital-output coefficient – the investment-efficiency rate (marginal rate of return from capital), the rate of profit, and the rate of interest – with the economy's growth-rate – under optimum. The rates of investment efficiency and of interest have shown themselves inherent in the dynamics of the price system – yet another facet of 'embedded' properties. Indeed, the same argument which elucidates the nature of price over time does so with respect to the rates of interest and of normative efficiency of capital throughout the economy. They put the same thing in a different way – the dynamic 'dual' provides a time-scale of the price system: it quantifies the changes over time.

Two further lines of development are noticeable; one towards perfecting the 'norm' of efficiency. Once the nature of the time-parameter and its inherently dynamic character have been understood, an element of inexorable uncertainty about future time had to be introduced. If anywhere it is here that a probabilistic treatment was imposed by the logic of the matter. Not only did the rate of interest then gain a safe place in planning theory and practice, but the theoretician came to distinguish what might be termed the 'core', call it the 'pure' return on capital and the superimposed element of risk entailed in the very passage of time in the uncertain world. Conceptually the formation of the 'normative' rate has come closer and closer to the market-formed one.

The explorations in the field have resulted in the feeling that planning theory is now ready to provide practice with the method of getting rational prices – in substance 'shadow' prices – for the productive factors. Clearly this of itself has seemed an immense step forward in re-equipping the planner with dependable tools.

The other line of development has been in the opposite direction – that of 'de-sophistication'. For while the programming approach has clarified the substance of the efficiency notions we mentioned, the algorithmic and computational requirements involved in its idealized implementation have proved too heavy. Hence the attempts in Soviet mathematical literature to design a tractable way of getting some 'efficiency norm' sufficiently approximating the ideal and not intractable. Significantly for the tendency, it is Kantorovich himself – jointly with Vainshtein et al. – who has produced the model for this kind of normative parameter.[35] In this particular model the rate, unique for the economy, is obtained from a simple, Cobb-Douglas-type production function sufficiently dynamized – allowing for advance in technology, gestation periods of capital goods, and their physical wear-and-tear and obsolescence. This alone tells us that the 'norm' – thus thought to be possible in the planner's practice – is incomparably superior to its pre-mathematical antecedent – in both quality and quantification. Yet not unlike the traditional 'efficiency norm' it is not derived from a formal, explicit optimization. Curiously, then, we are back in some respects to optimization 'behind the scenes' (see above); here too realism has clipped perfectionism.

Setting the plan's horizon

(13) Abandoning the static model in planning has confronted the theoreticians and practitioners with some extremely difficult issues. (In fact some of them are akin to those encountered in 'modelling' growth in an unplanned, competitive economy – a subject which has accumulated a vast literature in the West.) Some of the most complicated stem from the question of placing a 'horizon' on the plan. There is in this some kind of inherent contradiction. On the one hand the planner has naturally to think in terms of some 'terminal' time-point – whether he forms a 'traditionalist' or a mathematically stated plan. On the other, in real life an economy does not stop at any time-point: this makes in some sense for the artificiality – and in any case arbitrariness – of the time-horizon. The matter links up with some decisive elements of strategy – the setting of the rate of investment in the first place. Two schools of thought have developed in Soviet planning theory.[36] In spite of the 'artificiality' of any horizon, some stick to the idea that this is inevitable; the obvious consequence of putting a time-'ceiling' on the plan is the question of the so-called 'tail,' i.e. determining the volumes and pattern of output necessary for the economy's development beyond the plan period. Those who want such a 'ceiling' demand that the plan period should be sufficiently long since – so they reason – the longer it is, the less is the 'tail' to be dealt with (as the reader will easily notice, the approach of Kantorovich to 'perspective' planning sketched out above comes into this class). They argue also that changes in technology will in any case demand changing or adjusting the long-term plan some time mid-stream. But when? – that is the pertinent question asked by their opponents in the controversy. The latter maintain that the greater the length of the plan period, the greater the complications; they do not want to have any fixed plan period; for them the optimality criterion should be just the speed in reaching some targets – it is time that would be the 'minimand'. Planning with 'infinite' horizon is gaining support from some theorists.

The difficulties encountered in fitting in the time factor into plan-programming have stimulated the rethinking of the mathematical methodology as related to changes in Soviet strategy for growth. On this point, too, some ideas gestating in the TsEMI will be of interest. In them long-run planning is conceived of as organizing the movement of the economy towards some optimal steady-state progress; at each time-point the economy would be thought of as oriented towards a foreseeable and achievable state – and the path determined accordingly. As the conditions would change,[37] the state and the path would be adjusted; and so on. This approach has again entailed rethinking on the matter of the optimality criterion. It should be devised so as to secure the most effective transition to the steady-state regime: this being the 'idealized' state, the quality of the system's movement would be measured by deviation from the steady-state regime. Thence the idea of the best transition as the one for which the integral of deviation for the whole period is the smallest. (I would point to a certain affinity between the TsEMI thinking and that of the Cambridge school.[38] In the approach of Richard Stone and his associates – in their binary model of economic growth – we have two parts: one concerned with the long-run steady state, the other with the problem of adjusting the economy during the transitional period so as to meet its initial conditions, which is the short-run 'transient' sub-model.)

At the same time Soviet mathematical planning theory has turned for conceptual help to areas of scientific inquiry concerned with optimizing the point-to-point path or 'trajectory' – over time and stage-by-stage solution. In the present writer's view this new search, still far from any definitive results, merits consideration because of the hopes pinned on it.

Groping towards a 'cybernetic' portmanteau; assimilation of control theory; Optimality Principle and Maximum Principle

(14) The theoretical search to which we propose to turn now is oriented towards modern theories of system behaviour – in Soviet parlance, towards 'cybernetics' in the widest sense, and in particular to the theory of control and related disciplines. These are the areas of study originally developed from the angle of natural sciences – physics in the first place, thermodynamics, mechanics, and biology, but also engineering. The similarities of the working of an economy and a plant have been noticed in recent years by students in both East and West. It is the obsolescence of the traditional techniques in handling the problem of the plan, partly owing to its growing complexity, that has been impelling the control engineer towards these novelties,[39] and this now influences the economist, specifically the theoretician of planning. The working process of the plant has been aptly described as usually shaped by some independent and dependent variables and disturbances, and the substance of the optimum control of this process has been described as manipulation of the first-named so as to get the best output notwithstan-

ding the fluctuations brought about by disturbances.[40] Patently the 'manipulation' – in the sense used – has a closer analogy in a planned than in a non-planned economy; and in fact the closest analogy in a normatively planned one. This is so although one should not lose sight of its limitations: even the central normative planner and the control engineer should not do so; the latter if only because he normally has a range of alternatives – to begin with, in structuring the plant, so as to make it as controllable as possible. The possibilities of the architect of a normatively planned economic system are naturally even much more circumscribed. This granted, a good deal of the theory built up with an eye to plant control, including that of feedback systems, adaptive and self-controlled systems, and so on, has proved assimilable for planning theory and practice.

The mathematical apparatus to which the novel disciplines have turned has been basically that of the calculus of variations. However, the time-honoured method of calculus has not proved adequate to deal with the problem. (In particular, what would seem to be the obvious procedure – usually called that of enumeration – is more often than not precluded by the sheer size of the problem. There are also various technical snags on which we cannot elaborate here: one is that owing to the nature of the real-world problem, the character of the constraints results in the solution being a boundary point of the region of variation.) In the face of these obstacles, some 'non-classical' mathematical methods, mainly evolved in the mid-twentieth century in the modelling of optimal control, have been resorted to. It may be remarked that here too Soviet scholarship has felt itself to be on a familiar ground; indeed some basic elements of the mathematical apparatus in this field are owed to the decisively important Russian-Soviet contributions: it is sufficient to mention the theory of stability the origins of the theory of regulation in Vyshnegraskiy, with its modern roots in Chebyshev and Lyapunov; the theory of oscillations in Mandelshtam and Andronov; the theory of probability in a system's motion in Markov; and the fundamentals of the apparatus in Kolmogorov, and so on.

Again, because of the complexity of the formalization, nothing more than some very broad indications of the new method's substance can be presented in this informal account. Of these methods two in particular, one designed in the Soviet Union by Pontryagin and his school, the other designed by Bellman and his school, have attracted the attention and interest of the theoretician of economic planning and understandably so, concerned as he is with the handling of controlled systems.[41]

In fact, Pontryagin's theory was originally addressed to the engineer rather than the economist, as has been most of the apparatus, as we have stated (it came to the notice of the planning economist only in the 1960s). Its guiding idea is the way of maintaining the controlled 'object' – we can say the plant's or the economy's mechanism – in the required regime of behaviour. Its key is the 'Maximum Principle': as defined by

Pontryagin, it determines the corresponding point-'chain' of controls and of the trajectory under optimum and reveals the optimal entailed *dynamized* price (as the Hamiltonian multiplier). Its common-sense meaning has been incisively described by Chang: 'If you wish to get there fastest give it the mostest'.[42] (We think that even a non-specialist will also grasp the geometric interpretation of the Principle, which is roughly that what is sought is the maximum projection of the speed on the direction.)

To Bellman[43] is owed the theory of dynamic programming. The label of programming should not confuse the reader: while it deals with the optimization – and does so over time – its basic approach differs in something more than its dynamics only from that of the classical programme, with which we were concerned before (though, as the advancing inquiry suggests, the formalizations are in principle reducible to each other, which is true of programmes and optimal controls in general). Its essence is the 'Optimality Principle': whatever the initial state of the system and the initial solution, subsequent solutions – each phase of the motion – should determine optimal strategy with respect to the state into which the system has been brought. A simpler verbal explanation can hardly be given than that offered by Bellman himself; and it is this. Rather than determining the best sequence of decisions from a fixed state, one does this at any state: this permits one to understand the very structure of the solution. A good 'conversational' common-sense restatement of this principle can be found in Feldbaum:[44] run as quickly as you can over each segment of the route; or, which comes to the same, try to cover a maximum possible distance in each time-interval: then clearly – we shall note – the whole of the time and route of your running will take care of itself; but, as Feldbaum pointedly says, the secret of a wise runner is to try to economize his strength bearing in mind his ultimate goal. Therein lies the problem, which is one of the sequence of optimizations under the Optimality Principle, which appears rather deceptively simple.

Not much more will, and probably can, be said in this brief account to explain the two Principles. But what has been said is enough, we believe, to suggest how naturally they cope – at least conceptually – with what is the very essence of the planner's job. That is why in our submission they are significant for the further stage of the revolution with which we are concerned.

Moreover, each of the Principles and of the methods of application – the algorithms – built up on them has certain properties most attractive to the planning theoretician and practitioner. A very major one is that they do reduce the dimensions of the problem by reorganizing it. And another is that they are a certain help – in some cases – in evading the hurdles of nonlinearity. More, the dynamization of the 'shadow' price would seem to have brought the concept of 'invisibly' running a socialist planned economy to its definitive conclusion. In fact the claim has been put forward for Pontryagin's construct that it indeed has superseded Adam Smith's famous idea by offering a new and a more powerful principle of the 'invisible hand.'

Shifting from deterministic to probabilistic attitudes

(15) But there is yet another property on which we feel we should say more at this rather late stage of our story. It is the problem of dealing with uncertainty. As hinted here more than once before, the lack of certainty is in fact the planner's inseparable companion. It is inseparable even when he builds up a 'static' plan – because of the never perfect data at his disposal. But it is *a fortiori* and self-evidently so when he moves from the planning statics to those of dynamics. Note that the traditional stand of Soviet planning doctrine has always been strikingly deterministic. This is yet another feature which we feel can be related to both the strategy dominating in the past and to the poverty of the means in the planner's technical arsenal, rather than (as usually interpreted) to a doctrinal dogma. The attitudes have greatly changed in recent years. The concept of the planner's 'infallibility' – consequential upon the deterministic stand – is definitely being abandoned. Planning is now understood to call for a proper combination of deterministic and probabilistic elements. A school of thought will argue that the economic system, including the one normatively planned, operates under the influence of random events; they would typically include on the one hand such phenomena as e.g. materialization of technical progress in the perspective of geophysical processes; but on the other generally human behaviour. This is yet another area of cognition where some traditional inhibitions could be overcome only gradually. We have in mind in particular the 'anti-subjectivist' inhibition; but by now we can read in the pages of Soviet theoretical inquiries the tenet that – along with the conception of logical probability – one has to recognize that of subjective, no less than that of objective, probability (the subjective, it is pointed out, develops within the framework of the Bayesian decision theory and the Bayesian theory in turn corresponds to the logic of modern man-machine systems).[45]

Once this view is taken, the problem of plan optimization is conceded to be, to a considerable extent, one of prediction – this too amounts to a change, of revolutionary significance, in Soviet planning thought. And again this change can easily be linked up with the development of new techniques. Thus we have elsewhere pointed to the intrinsic link between the solution of a linear programme and the game-theoretic solution: and methods have been elaborated for programming under uncertainty – uncertainty which may affect the criterion and/or the constraints. Games with imperfect information suggest themselves, in the context, as a helpful vehicle in the treatment of the planning agency's problems.

But some of the control-theoretic methods assimilated over the past decade or two by economics have the probabilistic approach inherent in them. Take the Bellman method: it has inherent in it the Markovian[46] elements. For the Markovian chain is such that the probability distribution for the states at any time-point of the future (state-to-state transition probability), where the present state is unknown, is 'unaffected' by the system's history and is considered dependent only on current situations. (Naturally, in the general case of uncertainty the past has to be allowed for.) Thus the nexus of the Bellman and the Markov approaches is, as we say, immanent in both: and both correspond to the usual approach of the constructor of a plan. The probabilistic approach has been elaborated, in Soviet and Western literature, for the Optimality Principle; and some noteworthy probabilistic formulation of the Pontryagin problem of 'pursuit' – the planning theoretician could say pursuit of the goal – has been attempted (there is an interesting differential-game-theoretic formulation of Pontryagin's method by himself).[47]

However, even some of the relatively well mastered theoretical elements of the methodologies we have mentioned here come up against very great difficulties in application. The mathematical formulation (in partial differential equations) of the Bellman principle is itself a source of such difficulties: one of the troubles with the Pontryagin principle is the absence of generally dependable ways of finding the initial point for the solution of the adjoint system of multipliers (in our context, interpretable as prices over time) the construction of which it requires. Both methods, though not in the same way in the same aspects, are computationally fairly involved, the difficulties fast becoming formidable as the problem's complexity increases: the burden of long chains of complex computations minimizing functions of several variables, integration, and so on: the size of the computational task as often as not defeats the purpose of application in planning. Hence the growing accent on methods of approximation – of solving the plan problems by simplified procedure with some degree of exactness. One among those noteworthy for our purposes is that produced by Feldbaum[48] in his model of 'dual control' and his synthesis of an adaptive – 'self-teaching' – system.

The plan's size and optimum; towards a theory of complex large-scale systems

(16) As pointed out here, in almost every context a very major source of trouble in the practical implementation of the mathematical constructs in planning (apart from heavily aggregated strategic planning) is the problem's size. We have seen how the 'curse of dimensions' affects the handling of what (to recall our point) is the particular case of the programme – with the optimality choice-making taken out of it. It stands to reason that this 'curse' is multiplied when the choice-making is put into it. Hence the interest in the theory of the complex large-scale system.

The matter of dealing with the problem of size is usually related – in economic literature – to that of devolution in decision-making, and more specifically, to that of decentralization in planning. There is often some confusion in such thinking; we shall try to indicate its source presently.

At this stage we will refer ourselves to the fundamental invention which is owed to Dantzig and Wolfe.[49] It rests on what is known as the decomposition principle (and the decomposition procedure, or algorithm). The name is due to the idea of 'breaking up' the economy into some parts – let us call them for short 'firms' – with some central co-ordinator at the top. Suppose we start with each firm coming forward by submitting to him a bill of goods, made up of its proposed outputs with supporting inputs. These must be made mutually feasible, and also compatible with the state of resources and demands external, to the system. In carrying out this job, the co-ordinator works out a system of valuations – call them 'prices' (remember what has been said about the prices embedded in a plan programme) – for each item of the bill, say plus a premium for the firm that just achieves a balance. This is notified to all engaged in the operation and they are exhorted to offer a new feasible programme at a lower cost for which an incentive may be offered. The co-ordinator combines the new offers with the early ones so as to secure a new balance (again with allowance made for external balance) – and issues a new set of prices and premia, and so on. This procedure is repeated – until it is found that no new offers are forthcoming for the improvement of the plan: this point can be thought of as that of the iterations' 'convergence' to the best solution, the optimum in quantities and price. One will realize at once – and indeed Dantzig and Wolfe themselves pointed this out in their celebrated paper – that the procedure can be looked upon as a game. (Formally the prices generated by the co-ordinator's programme induce the firm to look for the pure sub-programme analogue in a game-theoretic exercise.)

This idea underlies iteration procedures designed in Hungary by Kornai and Liptak, and in the Soviet Union by Volkonskiy.[50] Recent years have seen considerable expansion – in depth and width – in the field opened up by the classical Dantzig-Wolfe inquiry. Various approaches have been developed and formalized within both the programming and the control-theoretic framework. Some outstanding works on decomposition have been published within either of these two frames in the Soviet Union. Very significant attempts have been made in fact in Soviet writing to build up a general theory of decomposition (or the 'method of blocks', as it is termed): two such attempts deserve to be singled out – those by Polterovich[51] and by Pervozvanskiy and Pervozvanskaya.[52] The generalizations have advanced to the point of an attempted, and indeed not unconvincing, build-up on this basis of a general mathematical theory of planning.

The widest experience in the application of decomposition procedures has been accumulated by the Hungarians, who started by using the game-theoretic type of such a procedure. This had to be abandoned because it proved to be erratic; so too had the original Dantzig-Wolfe method because of its slowness; eventually the Hungarians found they had to content themselves with a simplified version of it. It is still far from certain that a practicable, adequate answer to the problem of size of the plan task – and speed in dealing with it – has been found, immense as the heuristic contribution of the Dantzig-Wolfe method undoubtedly is.

Demonstrably, the solution is closely connected with the matter of effectively organizing the flow of information, of its channelling and processing. Mathematical-economic modelling apart, the connecting aspect has also its computational side. (A noteworthy attempt to tackle this is the Kronsjö model of planning by 'linked computers'.)[53]

Optimality conditioned by information system; new awareness of problems

(17) While understanding of the significance of the nature of the price signal in the effective decision-making processes is by now enhanced by a vast body of theoretical work as well as empirical inquiry, that of the information system still lacks this support. The theoretical exploration of the matter, which is still very young, has family affiliations with control (see above).

Some students of the problem as it is faced by a socialist economy (that is, as one which, by contrast with the capitalist one, has no *a priori* 'bias' with respect to the question of the market versus non-market systems) would be inclined to adopt, as the criterion for the appraisal of the effectiveness of the mechanism, the relative cost of information in its optimal decision-making processes. It is almost a truism to contend that, *ceteris paribus,* one should choose as more economical that mechanism for which the cost is at minimum. However, firstly, the clause of *ceteris paribus* may as often as not undermine the criterion; secondly, not much more than some basic propositions have so far been built up with respect to cost tendencies of alternatives:[54] such as, for instance, the fact that the cost tends to rise disproportionately with the mass of circulating and processed information; and that, other things being equal, this mass tends to rise with the degree of concentration of data, vertical and horizontal, though even the second proposition would certainly call for qualifications. Worse still, there is the difficulty in real life in determining the method of 'true' cost-and-benefit valuation of information. The table reproduced gives an illustration of the very broad methods which are being worked out at present in Soviet literature on the subject.[55]

The underdevelopment of this domain of inquiry stands in sharp contrast with the generally agreed view that one should find ways of coping with the principal stumbling-block in the advance of mathematical methods in planning. The plenary meeting of the Soviet Academy's Research Council unanimously declared at its meeting in February

1969 that 'the optimization of all-economy plans and models and the employment of computational technology are impossible without their

Evaluation parameter	Value	Weighting coeff.	Product	Topicality coeff. t	Credibility coeff.	Accessibility coeff. a	Value V of information unit D
1. Significance	S	α	Sα				$V_{Di} = (S\alpha$
2. Usefulness	P	β	Pβ				$+ P\beta + Uf$
3. Employability and periodicity	Uf	γ	UF				$+ L\delta)$ tra
4.	L	δ	Lδ				

organic integration with the process of the plan construction itself, with the technology of planning'. And further on:

the prerequisite of such an integration is the fundamental change in the method and organization of planning; and also of processing information for the needs of all-economy planning as the first step towards [such an] integrated system. The creation of the system makes a vast and complex task which should be carried out according to a single plan within a clear organizational framework: this is so inasmuch as what is involved is nothing less than designing and putting to work one of the largest man-machine systems. Both can be achieved only by phasing [the advance] with practice gradually shifted to the advanced operational regime. . . .[56]

(The envisaged gradualism of the process well reflects the present mood of those concerned with the mathematization of Soviet planning, sobered by their experience.)[57] If so, the rapporteur at the May 1969 conference on automized systems of plan computation argued: until now it was believed that raising national income depended on the expansion of capital stock, correct use of labour resources, and equipping them with electric power; now one could legitimately add to this also the country's 'information equipment'.[58]

It has been pointed out that one of the first tasks faced is the co-ordination of the system of indicators employed by the various statistical, financial, and planning agencies and the elaboration of an 'information-normative basis' for the Gosplan's ASPR (automated system of plan computations). The lack of cohesion of the mass of information travelling in the various information channels is the major handicap of the existing system. However, the organic welding of the system presupposes an effective decomposition in space and time of the all-economy problem, and we have seen its difficulties. Conceivably a drastic rise in the powers of computational equipment would bring relief with respect to the size of the tractable problems; but it would not by itself solve other difficulties, especially those related to problems of the heterogeneity of the money and physical-term calculation and its integration.

Information system and decentralization: the interconnection

(18) Before we leave the subject of parametric signals and information generally, let us try to clarify – as promised – its relation to decentralization. We may start by pointing out that when the Hungarian school first presented their (game-theoretic) version of the Dantzig-Wolfe method, they argued that what is the substance of their two-level (subsequently extended to multilevel) planning merely formalizes the traditional planning of socialist countries. And, we would say, it really does so – conceptually. For conceptually, the Soviet-type central planning authority, the 'Gosplan' – under the direct centralist regime – is supposed to fix the quantities, and values, of its plan items by exchanging the information with the lower, executive, levels. This is the substance of what is usually described in Soviet textbook presentations as 'planning and counter-planning'. (The fact that – as pointed out – with the traditional means at hand the planners can hardly ever comply in their practice with what the textbooks demand from them does not affect the underlying basic concept itself.) We can thus see that conceptually the tool can be aptly placed at the service of a centralized – to be specific, directly centralized – variant of planning of the kind of which Soviet-designed planning is the prototype. But it does also provide a tool for what on our definition is the *indirect* variant of centralism – for it 'idealizes' a perfect mechanism for the generation of price signals – ultimately co-ordinated with the centre's goal (its objective function) for the steering of the economy. (It may be of interest to note that among the various models of decomposition we have just mentioned, at least one Soviet-designed one could, if practicable, secure a relatively high degree of devolution: in it prices are being 'matched' directly between the 'buyers' and 'purchasers', by-passing the centre. The planner imposes only one parameter – and generally the flow of information along the vertical axis of system is very modest.)

So our next question is – has the mathematical revolution in Soviet economics strengthened the devolutional tendencies? This is a question not easy to answer by a simple 'yes' or 'no'. The issue of devolution was fought and refought in the 1920s, and as a result some anti-devolutional bias has been evolved (in this respect the situation is different in other socialist countries). There has never been much interest in the Soviet Union in the Langovian-type of 'market socialism'. As we have argued, theoretically at least, the mathematical school has introduced the idea of the 'market versus the computer' as the alternatives. But the most recent years have seen something like an anti-devolution as well as a devolutional inclination among the mathematically oriented. For this train of thinking the stand of Academician Rumyantsev – put forward in the debates on the reform of Soviet economic mechanism – is noteworthy. Having acknowledged the benefits of efficient price-term calculation in central planning, he sounded a caveat against the ideas of those economists who 'naively' believe that a planned steering of the economic processes can be ensured by means of indirect regulation. From this – he went on to argue – there is only a short step

to accepting the idea of the possibility of controlling the development of a socialist economy by means of a market mechanism, which would mean in practice abandoning the principle of central planning and would inevitably lead to disproportions – an unproductive use of material and labour resources.[59]

Perhaps we might also point to certain ideas on the general trend in this field. Thus one of the Soviet academics who can be credited with inculcating in contemporary Soviet economics the idea of the equivalence of solutions in the optimal calculation and in perfectly competitive markets, Volkonskiy,[60] has come forward with an argument on the change in this trend: typically (he would argue) the decentralistic tendencies in American giant corporations noticeable from the 1920s onwards have been reversed in the 1950s – as a result of the rapid advance in mathematization and computerization. (In drawing the implied lesson for socialist planning countries, one must clearly bear in mind that the capitalist giants obtain a more or less effective pricing from the market.)[61]

Information network and automated-planning network; vision of ultimate ASPR

(19) Our last few paragraphs have broached the theme of what is termed 'automated' planning: it belongs to the vision of the final phase of mathematical planning. A few words on this subject.

The early 1970s saw the formulation of the working principles of the ASPR[62] – 'automized' system of plan computations – a name which carries a deliberate understatement for the man-machine system which is ultimately to take over the function of planning the national economy – to take it over 'completely' and at all levels. Its basis is postulated now to be a synthesis of past planning experience with modern mathematical-economic models and computational technology. This new stress on the 'intergrational' approach reflects the diagnosis of the mistakes which have been made. As diagnosed now, the essence of these mistakes is that, on the one hand, attempts have been made to put into practice mathematical-economic models without consideration as to whether and how they could be fitted into the present planning regime and its system of performance indices; and that, on the other hand, in consequence, modern means of computation, employed within the framework of traditional 'non-optimizing' planning, could not work efficiently.

These heart-searchings interestingly reflect both the ambitious goal and the experience in pursuing it.

The ASPR has what appears to be its microeconomic extension, the ASUP (initials of the 'automized' control system of an industrial enterprise'). While the 1965 all-Union conference on the same theme had aired concern because hardly any enterprise was able to claim, at the time, a 'correct and scientific' experiment, the 1971 successor had apparently before it a survey of a large number of ASUP's, in actual operation, throughout the country. This again brought some disappointments, as well as better insight into the nature of problems confronted. A major disappointment concerns the scope for the 'typified' automized unit. 'We have passed [so Fedoronko observed in 1972] the phase of *the primitive conception of the ASUP* [italics in the original] as implying elaboration of some kind of universal schema and its subsequent mechanical spreading to enterprises.'[63] Experience has taught those responsible for the project that the designs must be sufficiently individualized. Further development is expected to proceed on three levels: level (1) encompasses the functions of everyday management of operational planning and regulation; level (2) problems which have already been solved theoretically but not in practice; level (3) problems which still await theoretical solution. In actual fact, as implemented, i.e. on level (1), the system is reduced to not much more than dealing with traditional planning and regulating: as often as not, to simply speeding up these processes and securing their greater precision. Symptomatically for appreciation of the advantages in a parametric type of planning, the emphasis is on treating the ASUP unit – in design and experiment – as a *'financial-economic'* system. To cite again our source, what is needed is to deepen the knowledge of an enterprise as an 'organic integration of subsystems – productive-technological, financial-economic, social-psychological'.[64] There is a strong demand for models testable in computer simulation.

Optimal computation and theories of alternative mechanisms. Price-steered systems

(20) We may now take up the issues raised in the preceding sections and ask ourselves in a more general fashion: tremendous as is the contribution of the mathematical school to Soviet economics (on this more in the next section), has it by now offered a feasible alternative to the traditional mechanism, or a prospect of one?

Let us, to begin with, take what usually appears to be the most radical step – towards the alternative of a market system. This issue too has quite a long story – in Western thought, going back to Barone in the beginnings of the century.[65] However, the classical conceptions of market socialism have not been clear enough as to its nature. Perhaps that of Dickinson[66] is relatively the least vulnerable to such criticism: as far as one can see, he was thinking, even if only in a vague fashion – of an economy where the market would perform functions quite similar to those it does under capitalism, that is shaping the crucial economic proportions – consumption, capital formation, and so on – through the interplay of supply and demand. Vagueness of the model's shape apart, it has implications – social as well as economic, to mention only those related to wealth distribution – which, at least as yet, do not seem acceptable to socialist societies. In the most famous variant – that designed thirty years ago by Oskar Lange[67] – the market is thought of as the computing mechanism, with the central planning authority entrusted with the functions of checking, adjusting, and promulgating solutions evolved.

While the Dickinsonian variant would mean a more dramatic change in the socialist economic system than those that have been operated so far in practice, it is not dependent on the kind of 'revolution' which is the subject of this book. By contrast, the 'revolution' has a more immediate significance in the Langovian order of ideas.

We may return here to the striking conceptual implications of the discovery of plan-programming. It is the equivalence of the programming solution with the theory-of-games solution, found at the 'saddle-point', which, to put it in other terms, is equivalent to the ideally competitive market equilibrium. Thus in principle the programming methodology does provide a fully dependable substitute for the market. Why then employ the market rather than use the computer plus the programming algorithm? Lange[68] put this question to himself thirty years after the appearance of his celebrated paper. His answer is broadly this. It will be granted that, as between the two, the market is an obsolete instrument belonging to the pre-electronic era; it is affected by all kinds of weaknesses, lack of informational and operational precision, and slowness, possibly resulting in fluctuations and non-convergence. Moreover, it is likely, in practice, to have undesirable effects on income distribution; above all, the market is static. All this granted – Lange continued – the market is still preferable to its rival, the computer: for powerful as is the latter, it could not, at least could not as yet, cope with either the size or complicated interrelationship of elements of the real-world economy. Lange's precept (in his work of the 1960s) is to leave the statics to the market, while employing the computer, that is the programme-type computation – for dynamics – for the construction of the 'perspective' plan. That, Lange contended, was the answer to the argument of Hayek and Robbins of the 1930s.[69] The market would be in charge of solving the system of static simultaneous equation – through familiar iteration, trial-and-error type tâtonnement.

As we see it, Lange's position of the 1960s fails to elucidate the trickiest matter in the idea of using both 'rivals': it is the integration of the continuously produced static solution and the dynamic one – 'inserting' the dynamic parameters into the market. To put it very simply, the core of the problem is the enforcing of the planning centre's dynamic choice; we leave aside here how far the static choices *per se* can be acceptable to the centre. (Sir Roy Harrod[70] has argued that under socialism a 'normative' – otherwise termed 'natural' – price must be calculated and promulgated. In an interesting argument he points out that already in Adam Smith we have the distinction between the 'natural' and the 'market' price, the former epitomizing the action of the capitalists maximizing their private profit. Whether the comparison is valid or not, the point would seem valid for socialism – in our context.)

Note. The relative workability of alternatives corresponding to what in my terminology would be direct and indirect variants of a mandatory planning system has been well analysed by a member of the Soviet mathematical school, Vishnyev.[71] The former alternative – in Vishnyev's terminology, the 'imperative' system of planning – could be modelled under these strong assumptions: all production 'normatives', i.e. technological coefficients, are known *a priori*; sufficiently manoeuvrable reserves of materials, products, and capacities are available; 'imperative' tasks are assumed to be carried out without special incentives; algorithms for numerical solution with adequate, detailed, aggregation are at hand. Against this, the second alternative – in Vishnyev the 'normative' system (the reader should be warned against confusion due to our different terminology!) – presupposes: firstly, sufficiently fast-convergent iterative methods to secure the consistency of the optimal plan and optimal valuations (prices *sensu largo*); secondly, incentives effectively inducing producers to decision-making in strict correspondence with the system of valuations; and thirdly, taking into account social consequences of decentralized decisions made in advance and suitably corrected.

As Vishnyev convincingly points out, a combination of the two has the advantage of flexibility but at the same time suffers from logical contradiction: the probability for the combinatorial method of getting into the space of optimal solutions is very small, although it rises with a method of sequential correctives. No socialist country has as yet – Vishnyev pointedly remarks – the practical experience for the build-up of an economic plan based entirely on an optimal model.

Vishnyev is no less convincing in appraising ideas of 'self-adjusting' systems wherein the centre would formulate only optimality criteria and regulatory 'norms' (prices, norms of efficiency, and so on) while the enterprises would determine for themselves the operative plans; in so far as the centre would not surrender the power of setting the basic proportions in the economy's advance, there arises the problem of coordination of the decision-making at various levels of the economic hierarchy.

(One would also note in passing Vishnyev's diagnosis of Soviet realities. It is this: the experience of the last few years indicates that the system of imperative planning comes up against increasing difficulties:

'while the difficulties are indisputable, it is not possible to say without empirical proof whether they are connected with the principle of imperative ['administrative'] planning or are rather conditioned by its being technically incomplete.')[72]

Evolving relativistic approach to price-guidance and implications; anti-equilibrium schools

(21) From whichever angle we approach the matter of effectively steering the economy, we see that, at least in the first approximation, it appears to resolve itself into the question of the centre's ability to set prices sufficiently close to optimum. Coming round again to this question, it may be fitting to quote on this the present-day view of the mathematical architect of the apparatus which has revolutionized Soviet economics:

The quality of economic calculation [Academician Kantorovich says] depends on correct pricing ...; this role is performed by the objectively conditioned valuations [the dual of the optimal plan programme – see p. 19]. If we could successfully embrace in one model all the commodities produced within the economy, it would be natural to adopt valuations corresponding to the optimal plan (subject to correctives connected with nonlinearity, dynamics, and other elements not allowed for in the programme). ... Since the optimal plan is, in principle, the best achievable under the conditions of a socialist economy, such prices would ... form, in principle, the best prices. Unfortunately it is in practice impossible to construct such a model because of the large size of the problem, the absence of sufficient information, and other causes. All models which can be achieved in reality must be aggregated to a greater or smaller degree – and on this basis, while making use of the aggregated valuations found in this way, the prices have to be evaluated in addition. Moreover, patently, in particular with respect to consumer-good prices, one will have to allow for extra-economic factors connected with considerations of a social and political order.[73]

As a matter of fact we could refer the reader to even stronger expressions of Kantorovich's present relativistic attitude:[74] in one of his recent contributions to the debate on the applicational potentialities of his method, he voices his doubts with regard to the idea of the uniqueness of the optimal plan. Realistically, he argues, one should only talk of a whole set of plans close to optimum: the choice could be made from among them 'in meeting conditions and requirements which do not lend themselves to formalization in an optimality criterion'.

Further, his most recent statements are illuminating also for some additional qualifications.

Such indicators as prices and their structure [he points out], depreciation (amortization) norms, rents related to limitations in natural resources, rentals on equipment, normative charges on productive assets, normative investment efficiency, charges or subsidies related to the use of some labour resources, profit and so on, have either been rigorously justified or revealed in the analysis of optimal-planning models.[75]

Yet, he adds, 'this system of indicators, presupposes, or corresponds to a particular type of organization of the economy's functioning', and this aspect has not been completely investigated as yet.

Of interest too should be the experience of socialist planning bodies. Since that of the Hungarian planners is particularly substantial, their general conclusion does carry considerable weight; and it is that the introduction of shadow prices as official prices – shadow prices obtained in the course of the programming – is not feasible. Here too as contributing elements are named the limited capacities of the programming apparatus, the lack of precision in the workable approximations of relations resorted to in the majority of cases for coping with non-linearities, and also the unsolved difficulties in the handling of uncertainties. It is incidentally interesting to note that the Hungarian findings suggest that central guidance, either by centrally-fixed prices or by direct orders, entails the collection and processing of roughly the same quantity of information. This is the argument which appears to be decisive with this Hungarian school of thought, which is now inclined to assume that guidance through a centrally-fixed price would be just as inefficient as that through direct command. Hence its support for the idea of relying on the market – though with the centre's 'influencing' of its processes ensured.[76] (We shall not repeat here our reservations as to the workability of this concept in a socialist planned system.)

Moreover, an influential Hungarian school of thought argues – on the theoretical plane – that price is neither the exclusive nor the principal instrument for the guidance of an economic system. Suffice it here to hint that this school of thought – the anti-equilibrium school, for which the writings of Janos Kornai are most representative – stresses its 'normative' stand which can be fairly described as 'anti-quietism'. To reproduce the main argument: while it is generally accepted in economics that the virtues of equilibrium are self-evident, strategically sufficiently strong pressures secure greater vigour to the economy: as defined in theory, equilibrium is a position of rest generating the tendency to non-disturbance, and that must lead logically to inertia: thus 'healthy' disturbance appears as more desirable than equilibrium, with logical consequences for the equilibrium price system.[77]

It is interesting to see how similar issues of activating 'pressures' and feedbacks have been approached by some Soviet theoreticians – in the framework of the Soviet economic mechanism. Trapeznikov[78] has argued that performance criteria of the controlling and operating levels should be integrated throughout the controlled system[79] forming, that is, an interlocked and non-self-contradictory whole; that 'game' situations should be taken advantage of as one of the most effective means to activate man's initiative; that the system should be operated under intensive 'feedback pressures', in particular, pressures from the user to the producer and from hierarchically lower to higher echelons.[80] On the last postulate, it has been observed that in general the problems of analysis, the selection of parameters when the shape of the function is determined, have by now received a deeper understanding and fuller elaboration than those of the synthesis of the 'laws' of feedback (Lyetov).[81]

Stock-taking in 'post-elation' phase

(22) Our concluding remarks on the use of mathematics in planning theory and practice will start with some references to Soviet stocktaking – a report on mathematical modelling submitted to the first conference on optimal planning and control of the national economy in December 1971. Its principal emphasis is on the partial character of the constructs, on their failure to treat the economy's complex interrelationships as one integrated whole. Their results – to continue the findings – have been 'impoverished' by drastic simplifications; in turn these are due to a poor informational basis. They have been weak in their 'systemic' approach; hence informational incongruity with the system of plan computations and disparity of dimensions. The conclusion is anything but surprising at the present 'post-elation' phase:[82]

there was an illusion (not quite abandoned even today) that mathematical methods are the key to solve all economic problems; and this has led to an exaggerated – or at least a wrong – 'measure of mathematization': of appraising the mathematical model's potentialities in planning and controlling the national economy at the present level of development of our scientific conceptions.

What then are these 'potentialities'? Faced with this question let us move straight into *medias res* and broach the fundamental matter, the subject of unending controversy – of the value of mathematics in the world of economics in general. One will certainly agree with those who argue that mathematical economics and econometrics are not the only disciplines providing those concerned with real-world economies – and with the business of planning them – with the necessary equipment. They have no monopoly in the field, but it seems safe to maintain that they do provide the method for the maximum – let us stress this, the achievable, relative, maximum of rigour in economic thinking. And the need for rigour in this field is, in our submission, rapidly increasing. Why is it so? On this point Domar[83] is very convincing: most present-day economic problems are too complex and entail too many variables with intricate interrelationships to be tractable without the help of mathematics. (We could move here to an even higher plane of generality and invoke Whitehead and Russell[84] for the argument that the adoption of symbolism in processes of deduction aids intuition in regions which

41

are too abstract for imagination – surely an invaluable property in the economist's reasoning.)

Moreover, there is good reason for expecting that in the further development of its 'language' mathematics will be more directly related to the need of economics than was the case in the past. Traditionally it was physics and mechanics that were placing 'orders' with pure mathematics for the supply of the necessary apparatus, the social sciences having to content themselves with whatever of it they could make use of for their purposes (and in fact, as the father of cybernetics remarked in the 1960s, the mathematical physics which social scientists employ for their models is that of the middle of the previous century).[85] But more recent developments would indicate in this respect a change in the status of economics – and in particular planning economics – *vis-à-vis* mathematics: the inspiration for work in some parts of the latter comes direct from the former. This point has been convincingly made by Academician Kantorovich, and it is certainly true of some of his own seminal contributions (and also, *inter alia,* of some parts of the mathematical control-theoretic apparatus – see above); parenthetically we may quote Oskar Morgenstern's persuasive view that just as mathematics has profited from having been tied so closely to the physical sciences, it now stands to gain from being deeply 'involved' with the social world.[86] In this context we may recall Kantorovich's related observation that it is only the mathematical apparatus that has been changing planning from an essentially qualitative into a quantitative exercise. (From the context it would seem that this was said with special reference to the Soviet-developed planning method. This judgement – tenable when properly qualified – would mean that in some sense the birth of planning as a sufficiently exact science and technique dates from the time of the assimilation of mathematics, for is not non-quantitative planning economics a contradiction in terms? Further, when accepting Kantorovich's point, one should avoid a pitfall: mathematizing economics by no means confines its usefulness to the quantification of processes. For as a matter of fact modern mathematics quite often helps insight into the qualitative aspects as well. (On this a good point is made by Hurwicz in referring to problems of consumer preferences:[87] it certainly has proved the non-quantitative nature of some economic phenomena. On the other hand it is topological analysis that has helped to obtain conditions permitting the numerical presentation of preference orderings.)

The Kantorovich proposition links up with the aspect of computational technology; once again we may point to the dramatic leap of Soviet planning from its 'five-fingers-plus-abacus' technique straight to that of the electronic computer. And note the potentialities: according to Herman Kahn,[88] defining the computer's power as the speed-times-memory product, the potentialities may be expected to increase during the 1970s by a factor of about 10,000.

This may be the right context for a few remarks on the interaction of the technology of computation and developments in the social sciences in general, and in the economics of planning in particular. On this Enders Robinson[89] in his observations points to something which seems to us extremely important, though it has escaped the student's attention. Its substance is that there are two most powerful directions of impact of the present state of the machinery on those sciences, but somewhat paradoxically, calculation *qua* calculation is not one of them. Rather they are simulation, and the construction of theory. The latter relates to the 'minimal' definition of theory offered and means an impact on methodology; and it is Robinson's exciting prediction that its impact, plus advances in contemporary logic and mathematical programming, are likely to change the very 'face' of theoretical thinking as such. With respect to the former, the paradox that the electronic computing machine (whatever were originally its designers' intention) has greater potentialities as a simulator than as a calculator is, in his view, no less remarkable. To put it briefly, the substance of the argument is that, being a simulacrum of experiment, simulation broadens the area – so very circumscribed in the social sciences – of experimenting in the wider sense, and thereby of empirically shaping or adjusted theorizing. (Two questions – and the way they can be answered by the student – pose themselves: one concerning the sense in experimenting, the other concerning the scope for building up a sufficiently 'economical' theory will not be enlarged upon here; but the effect on the perennial problem of the 'completeness' of the theory should be stressed.) There are fields of economic theory for which an adequate simulation of real-life processes seems to carry a particularly good promise; to give just one or two examples, there are some issues in the theory of decentralization and of the theory of growth where imitative procedures can help in providing something like a definitive answer.

The impact we have just discussed is as it were self-intensifying. For, to refer again to Robinson, once a formalization of a theory is given, we gain – for the investigation of its properties – the whole power of metamathematics. (All that has been said here holds pre-eminently for the control-theoretic approach to planning.)

Some of the limitations have roots inherent in any formal modelling of the real world. This is so because any formalization of it is condemned to selecting only *some* of the variables and functions which ideally should *all* come into its mathematical image. Selecting a few – but which ones? Or, to refer oneself to yet another of Bellman's perceptive obiter dicta,[90] one must bear in mind that real systems can and do have various mathematical realizations depending on their purposes, for the mathematical system is 'never more than a projection of the real system *on a conceptual axis*'.[91] This incidentally is one of the reasons why planning – formalized planning included – is a matter of art as well as science; and only in case of mathematically supported planning could we say as well, a relatively exact science.

Another point in the same order of thinking. Even the most successful idealization of the economic system – 'capturing' it in the language of symbols – leaves out, and inescapably must leave out, a certain qualitative 'residue'.[92] Indeed, coping with this extremely important and yet definitionally evasive 'residual' element is one of the handicaps the user of mathematical planning comes up against. Attempts have been made in Soviet literature to embrace some elements of this kind in some logical-analytic models and to co-ordinate them with the 'algorithmic' planning models.

This is yet another point at which we have at least to hint at the now most 'fashionable' system-theoretic tendencies. They seem to have dominated the intellectual climate at the 1971 Soviet conference on automatic control. Parenthetically, the development of the Soviet mathematical school in economics was synthesized there in three periods, i.e. those of (1) the emergence of the school in the second half of the 1950s at the tangency plane of economics, mathematics, and cybernetics; (2) its establishing its 'right' to exist, of 'assailing' the major problems of theory and practice – from the beginning till the late 1960s; and (3) the present phase, one of the most important characteristic features of which is the 'systemic approach'.

In anticipation of the Note on this approach (see p. 48), we wish to mention one factor – articulated in the 'systemic' approach by Pervozvanskiy,[93] himself a distinguished contributor to the advance of control-theoretic formalism. It is the presence of man as an element of control in the 'large system' – here was his stress – that is the cause of the observed fact that the formulation of the 'habitual' optimization problem and the evolving on this basis of an optimal-control programme fail to offer the expected yields. The requirements with respect to an optimum – from the human being's angle – by far exceed the potentialities of, and indeed are difficult to embrace in, the traditional framework; the great issue is the search for a framework which could handle this factor.

Limitations of mathematical techniques, or of planning *qua* planning

(23) To fundamental limitations of mathematical methodology as such, one would add the specific ones of methods and techniques so far placed at the service of economic planning. We have seen them virtually at every step of our story. Again and again we have pointed to the hurdles and barriers, most of them only very gradually relaxed or reduced but not sufficiently overcome – to recall those connected with the size of the problems, the shape of relations (nonlinearities), the trickiness of the impact of the time dimension (in fact spatio-temporal dimension) on them. We have stressed further the questions of their dependability and the general effect of uncertainty not only with respect to the future but also the present situation. (We have seen, in particular, the limitations affec-

ting also some of the new promising methods, such as those offered by theory of control and related disciplines.) It seems to be a not illegitimate supposition that in reality, more often than not, the various handicaps discussed do not occur in isolation: far from this, they have to be faced in complex and mutually complicating and intensifying combinations.[94]

But on the other hand it seems to us an equally defensible proposition that virtually every one of these handicaps is not really a specific weakness of the application of mathematics to economic planning, as the anti-mathematical school has been inclined to say. Surely the difficulties due to the size of the problems the macro-economic planner has to handle, the complexity of relationships, the poverty of informational data, the lack of sufficient certainty – all of them have been with the planner ever since the planning of economies has been attempted. The rigour of the mathematical method has only made the planner conscious of them and has precluded what one could perhaps call 'the reliance on impression' – on a sufficiently high degree of impression that is, which is in a peculiar sense the source of flexibility and manoeuvrability and in this sense the basis of viability – of the traditional method. Regarded in this way, the question of the workability of mathematical planning is largely one of the workability of planning, specifically normative planning *as such* – a matter on which we do not propose to pronounce. Parenthetically, nor do we find it useful to draw any conclusions from the degree to which original expectations of the impact of mathematical methods on planning practice have materialized. Undoubtedly, looking back, they have proved too optimistic: Kantorovich is on record with the view that shifting from the traditional to the more perfect techniques of planning and methods of calculation should bring about in a short time a very rapid increase of the Soviet national product. It detracts nothing from the brilliance and historical greatness of his discoveries that this has not been borne out by reality.

Beneficiaries of revolution: theory or application? Profound change in Soviet economics

(24) Which has been the great beneficiary of the assimilation of mathematics in Soviet economics, and in particular in planning economics – the theory, or the applicational branches? The answer is probably – both. Most recent Soviet sources claim that

already at the present stage of development of Soviet mathematical-economic science one can elaborate, in a short time, a complex of machine-informational systems making it possible operationally to represent various social-economic situations, to appraise economic efficiency and to give a scientific basis to decision-making on most important problems of the country's development.[95]

But as it would seem to me, it is the cognitive impact that is the more decisive one. It is a fact that this has originally been confined to the area of planning technique, where immediate gains were expected. The process of reception, and the impact, were bound to widen and deepen. As a Soviet student of this impact has observed, 'the use of mathematics in economics, while dictated first and foremost by the needs of practice, calls for a revision of many a dogma, many an obsolete conception'.[96]

A related aspect is the changing attitude with respect to the intellectual self-sufficiency of socialist economics. Inevitably, where the fundamental and complete divorce of capitalist and socialist economics has been the accepted axiom for decades, the process is not without perplexing difficulties to the economist, who indeed in this deserves our understanding. Those who deal with such perplexities in Soviet literature would typically stress that[97]

formal universality, neutrality, of mathematical methods should not cover their misuse for the support of the artificial and harmful conception of a 'convergence' of capitalism and socialism, [for] econometrics does not support the characteristically reformist illusions, first of all the myth of the alleged inescapable rapprochement of the private-capitalist and the planned economies on the common platform of a mixed economy.

But at the next step of reasoning it is readily conceded that it is the formal kinship of models – specifically of macro-models for the structural analysis and prognosis of the economic system – that has legitimately induced the international exchange of ideas; to say nothing of methodology and algorithms for the numerical solution of a complex economic system which give scope 'for mutual information and scientific co-operation of the widest international aspect'. It is in our view this stand that deserves our attention: this stand rather than the exhortations to vigilance which are *de rigueur* in Soviet writing, or reservations to the effect that 'in substance the "convergence" is confined to the logical-mathematical formalism which is the common language of all sciences that have reached a given level of development',[98] – to conclude this citation from the distinguished mathematical-economic journal which has to be credited with great merit in the advancement of the process with which our study is concerned. (For the sake of balance in the picture we note that one could read in the pages of the same journal[99] a suggestion for 'three basic approaches' in the mathematical theory of economics, viz. the game-theoretic, which treats the economy as resulting from activities of subjects with individual objective functions; the Keynesian, i.e. one postulating a 'regulated market' with central prognostication of, and subsequent intervention into, the course of economic processes, even if confined to only a few aspects (fiscal, credit, foreign economic policies) and sectors; and the 'optimizing approach', introducing a centrally organized mechanism for economic decision-making in accordance with explicitly formulated social goals. (Whether or not this rather sweeping formulation is adequate, when presented as indicating the area of legitimate scholarly inquiry, it does reflect significantly the new climate.)

What seems to us most promising in the longer run is the fact that the insulation of Soviet theoretical thinking in economics has at last come to an end. Undoubtedly, mathematically formulated ideas, 'imported' from the West, have by now made a major contribution to the change in this thinking; it is a change in an amazingly short period, beyond any recognition: it is enough to recall, as examples, the formidable impact of the von Neumann–Morgenstern game-theoretic ideas and apparatus in general, or of Neumannian conceptions on the theory of planning growth, or the effect of Western writing, Bellman's on the theory of steering the economic system or e.g. Tintner's on the stochastic approach. The *two*-way channels of communication are at last open; the stress is on 'two ways', since one hardly needs to specify what contemporary Western economic theory owes to the Russian and Soviet mathematical genius, from Lyapunov and Markov onwards to Kolmogorov, Kantorovich, Pontryagin, et al. (The Soviet discipline I have in mind when talking about the end of insulation: it is 'economic economics'; 'political economy' has remained what it was: engrossed in its traditional hermetic exercises, it continues in its splendid isolation from modern thinking; but it now has hardly any relevance whatsoever for contemporary Soviet economic-theoretic thought in the accepted sense of these words.)

To sum up, the intellectual internationalization is, in our submission, one of the most important facets of the revolution which constitutes our theme. The mathematization of the science of economics – says the Soviet authority just quoted – is an irreversible process. So, one may legitimately expect, is the facet of its internationalization.

Notes. (1) As indicated, the growing sense of the limits of the assimilated mathematical apparatus for extremization, in serving the purpose of an 'optimized' economy, has in most recent years given a strong impulsion to turn for help to general system and information theory, both with a strong probabilistic basis; and also to seek ways of widening the theoretical foundations of planning theory and enriching the planner's box of tools by interdisciplinary borrowing. (One could possibly relate this to the view, attractive to the Soviet theorist, that a counterpart to progressive specialization is a parallel integration – on some 'upper planes' of generality – of fundamentals in sciences, production and education, and control systems,[100] as one of the features of the contemporary scientific-technological revolution. I have discussed this attraction elsewhere. Here I merely wish to indicate the significant impact of the tendencies alluded to on modes of thinking. At the centre of Soviet mathematical-economic explorations, it is now being maintained[101] that the specific environmental conditions of our era entail a very high factor of indeterminacy in planning. Hence – so it is maintained – rather than relying on formal methods, it is necessary, especially in 'perspective' planning, to combine such methods with an intuitive approach. It is precisely this that accounts for the attraction of the systemic methodologies to Soviet mathematical economists, and for their renaissance. We can thus observe something of a dialectical process: while powerfully propelling the replacement of intuitive decision-making by formal algorithms and numerical solutions, the computer tends at the same time to promote intuitive approaches in planning processes not fully resolvable in logical steps.[102] However, it seems valid to maintain that so far the system-theoretic orientation has brought certain cognitive gains rather than new practicable techniques.

(It may be noted that the new systemic approach is also gaining adherents in mathematical schools of other socialist countries. In this the Hungarian school, of which Kornai is the leading member, is noteworthy. [Compare with what was said on p. 40 and note the remarkable change in his stand.] Its arguments are based on both theoretical considerations and empirical observations. The former are related to Kornai's repudiation of the general-equilibrium approach, which makes his stand akin to that of Mikhalevskiy in Soviet writing: that approach, criticized as artificial and in particular as unrealistic because of its staticness, is replaced in Kornai by an explicit disequilibrium approach as fundamental in normative planning.[103] Of immediate relevance for economic planning is the conclusion derived, i.e. that an economic system cannot be efficiently operated when relying for guidance exclusively on price signals; that indeed in its signalling system price can play only a subordinate role. It is safe to say that the Soviet mathematical school has not followed this line in respect of the price mechanism; and that even those members of that school who – like Mikhalevskiy – share with Kornai the disequilibrium-theoretic stand do not go as far as he does in conclusions drawn from it.)

Our last point in this section of this note is drawn from analogy. Economic planning is not an isolated discipline. As a matter of fact it is its mathematization that has inspired and helped the detection of family relations; and developments in cognate fields may provide some relevant hints for the domain of our interest.

One such has recently been indicated by Academician Trapeznikov.[104] As he observes, in mechanics the systems of automatic regulation as traditionally evolved have proved insufficiently viable (largely because of some adopted assumptions). Hence the search – a successful one – for new methods of constructing controls for interconnected systems. The same – such is the argument of Trapeznikov – is in substance the basic problem of control-models for the economy: '[its] structure of controls which can secure sufficient flexibility must be worked out from the angle of the contemporary methods of automatic control' and 'naturally here only the experience accumulated with respect to systems of automatic controls in technical mechanics should be made use of'. (The extra-economic implications which such attitude may be found to entail fall outside the scope of this study and will not be discussed.) The channels of communication through which fertilizing ideas may be drawn from related disciplines is again the common mathematical framework.

(2) As now defined at the TsEMI, the principles of perspective planning – under the 'systemic' approach – would entail the following rules. (1) The central plan must always embrace some species of decompositional planning, assuming, accordingly, some multi-level iterative coordination process; (2) both medium- and long-run plans must be evolved in a multi-variant procedure; (3) all centralized planning must be based on a combination of algorithmic and heuristic elaboration. The higher 'floors' include what for a longer period (10–15 years) would be the

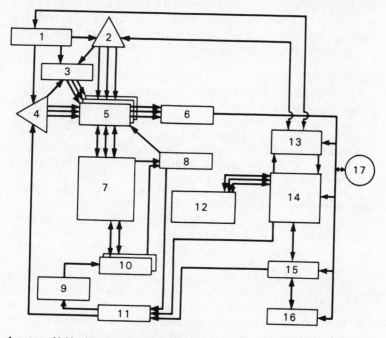

A system of 'objective-directed' plan models

1. Long-run forecasts; 2. Objectives. 3. Elaboration of programmes. 4. Resources. 5. 'Objective-oriented' programmes. 6. Requirements in resources. 7. Evaluation of programmes from the point of view of objectives and resources ('Efficiency of resource-uses'). 8. Adoption of programmes. 9. Elaboration of resource-programmes. 10. Resource programmes. 11. 'Complex-system' plan. 12. Models of sub-optimization, sectoral and regional. 13. Macro-models of overall optimization (national economy). 14. System of intersectoral and interregional models, including the intersectoral and interregional 'balance'. 15. Social balance of plans. 16. Extra-economic resources. 17. The system's operation.

Source: N. P. Fedorenko, in *EMM,* 4 (1971), p. 491.

'genplan' ('general plan'), based on social, economic, and technological forecasts. (For the last forty years Soviet planning has been hankering after a 'genplan'!) The perspective planning scheme designed at the TsEMI consists of two broad components: (a) a system of a balance-type plans providing a point of departure for the optimal national-economic plan, and (b) a system of 'direct' optimizing planning. So far only parts of the first-mentioned system have been elaborated. They form a complex system of blocks with a 'multi-cascade' control of various types of inter- and intra-bloc processes. It is open at each level; open in the sense that the 'boundaries' of the medium-term plan are conventionally a 'multi-cascade' control of various parameters and variables, and their continuous review. The same is true of the subsystems at each level, except that here the central planner intervenes with the parameters of the overall plan. Experimentally, for the 'level 1' (top level) of the system, so far, a full-cycle computation has been carried out for two successive five-year plans in several variants and has been tested on various hypotheses. Although the non-equilibrium school is represented in the TsEMI (see p. 48), the models are of a strongly equilibrium type.

Postscript

At the time that this book was being prepared for the press in late 1973 the principal Soviet journal published[105] a significant appraisal of certain developments and tendencies in the assimilation of mathematical-economic methodology (MEM). Because of the eminence of the journal and of the author (Dr Vishnyev is a distinguished scholar in our field), and because his diagnosis well illustrates some of the issues discussed here (and indeed supports some of our tenets), I wish to add the following very brief résumé of Vishnyev's main propositions and findings here.

It is scarcely necessary to dwell on the achievements of MEM in the build-up of a system of automated control, in the use of matrix balances in intersectoral relations for planning, in securing optimal location of industrial enterprises, in the choice of technological processes, of the most advantageous transport flows, and so on. But at the same time one hears voices – some, in fact, coming from the initiators of the MEM – expressing deep dissatisfaction with its application in practice. Thus the time has come for an objective appraisal of factors which at this stage constrain the potentialities of MEM. Some are immanent in the methodology itself, others are exogenous.

To start with the immanent, the development of MEM is far from complete and this alone tends to limit its present yields. Strictly methodology factors apart, one has to consider under this heading the difficulties in formalization and those relating to computational and technical problems, which as yet remain unresolved.

To be more specific as to the latter, important results have been obtained in the domain of formalized 'languages' and typology of models;

this is true in particular of system-theoretic analysis, goal-oriented approach, game-theoretic ideas, network and graph-theoretic modelling, theory of probability, theory of queueing, etc. It has to be admitted that these techniques and approaches, while productive at the level of an enterprise, branch, or region, have proved to be less so on a formalized all-economy dynamic plane. Quite possibly, then, what is needed here are some new, completely original ideas.

In this context one notes the good results of decompositional methods – methods based on a rational breaking-up of complex problems into subproblems and a subsequent re-composition of solutions. Here theory does respond well to the demands of practice, and elaborates on new approaches and solutions to the handling of complex structures. It has also become a widely acknowledged view that a vast class of complex social-economic and ecological problems lends itself to computer-imitation, which is in substance a statistical procedure plus models substituted for inaccessible experimentation. *Mutatis mutandis,* the same applies to heuristic strategies which aim at some adequate approximations where exact solutions appear to be unachievable.

It must be granted that the systemic approach to economic problems is so far more of a declarative than real nature. This is accounted for by the difficulties encountered in attempting to apply it to social phenomena. . . . Considerable effort will be needed to construct a system of interlinked models of the national economy . . . which would reflect the extremely intricate network of both direct and feedback flows of labour, products, and money of self-organizing and self-developing economic systems. . . .

In some sense the difficulties in prognostication are of a kindred character. Here the three classes of trouble, in ascending order, are those connected with (a) the identification of the laws of, and tendencies in, the system's transition from one state into another; (b) the detection, within the 'zone of indeterminacy', of the path of evolution; (c) the forecasting of the trajectory based on the system's postulated terminal state. While a good deal has been achieved, a large number of problems still awaits a solution. An important matter to bear in mind is that 'from the point of view of controllability, the economic system differs radically from the technological one. For in an economy one cannot rely on the lower echelon to carry out exactly and without reservations the commands of the higher agencies.'

Among the 'objective' extraneous factors, a relevant one is the level of an economy's development. The sterility of MEM in many countries is caused by the economic immaturity of these countries. On the other hand, in highly developed capitalist countries its effectiveness is circumscribed by the system's weak controllability on the macro level. This does not apply to the Soviet Union; but there are some underdeveloped sectors in the Soviet economy which do inhibit the application of MEM (these difficulties will be reduced only as these sectors advance). Moreover, an economy's maturity is related to its structure and organization; in the Soviet Union both are undergoing very rapid change. In the circumstances, the inertia of the planning and controlling apparatus is a cause of a lag in organizational advance: scientific principles find a slow reception in the economy, and this restrains a wide and productive adoption of MEM.

A lagging element in the Soviet economic reality is also that of informational services. Securing the required information comes up against certain difficulties. 'The forms of collecting and of processing information as they were evolved [in the USSR] lag behind the increasing demands of sciences.' Developing and improving the socio-demographic and economic information and reducing the lag in supplying it to the user is a task of first-order importance. Once again in this context the emphasis is on the elaboration of a suitable 'language' which would permit an effective use of the computer. (However, 'one cannot deny a certain inertia in some of the economic personnel which inhibits the assimilation of new methods'. An incentive-oriented mechanism should be one way of overcoming it.)

To put it in a nutshell, Dr Vishnyev's main conclusions may be restated as follows.

The process of assimilation of new ideas, theories, and paradigms quite often passes through four phases. The initial phase is one of indifference and disbelief. This 'zero' phase with respect to economic cybernetics was a prolonged one in the Soviet Union. It was so for a variety of causes:

... in particular owing to the erroneous identification of MEM with the mathematical trend in the bourgeois political economy. Yet it is harmful as well as erroneous to substitute for the struggle against bourgeois ideology the artificial idea of a collision between the traditional forms and mathematical methods in economics.

The next phase is that 'of a breakthrough in the wall of the lack of understanding and the distrust of the conceptions, and the start of their implementation . . .'; 'this is usually accompanied by exaggerated expectations of their practical effectiveness . . .'. That phase – the 'phase of enthusiasm' – is very often followed by a 'reaction': great hopes fail to materialize fully, difficulties and limitations appear, the impetus of new ideas loses its momentum; in this critical phase it is the sceptics who become most vocal.

'It is important to pass this phase without essential losses: a healthy theory emerges from the critical phase intrinsically strengthened and arrives at phase four – the phase of organic development – with a more powerful scientific and applicational potential.'

The scientific-technological revolution complicates the steering of a socialist economy extremely, but at the same time it puts the powerful instruments of mathematical methods and computation into the hands of the planners. Making full use of them should become part and parcel of the very-long-term plan of the country's economic development; and it calls for closer and closer collaboration between the Soviet planner and the scientist. In a word the moral is this: the mathematical revolution has presented an important opportunity. At the very difficult stage through which the economy is passing, the economist strategy-makers must take care not to throw that opportunity away.

Abbreviations

Avt. i tel.	*Avtomatika i telemekhanika*
EMM	*Ekonomika i matematicheskiye metody*
Plan. khoz.	*Planovoye khozyaistvo*
Q. J. Econ.	*Quarterly Journal of Economics*
R. Econ. Stud.	*Review of Economic Studies*
Vopr. ekon.	*Voprosy ekonomiki*

Notes and Sources

1 There are no copies of the original in the West, to our knowledge. There is a French translation: V. K. Dmitriev, *Essais économiques (Ricardo, Cournot, Walrus)* (Paris, 1968) and 'Presentation' by Alfred Zauberman; cf. also Zauberman, 'A few remarks on a discovery in Soviet economics', *Bulletin of Oxford Univ. Inst. of Stat.*, Nov. 1962.

2 And his previous works quoted therein.

3 A. Zauberman, 'Soviet work related to the von Neumann model and turnpike theories and some ramifications', in G. Bruckmann/W. Weber, eds., *Contributions to the von Neumann growth model* (1971); and George Morton/A. Zauberman, 'Von Neumann's model and Soviet long-term (perspective) planning', *Kyklos*, 1 (1969).

4 cf. in particular J. Hicks, *Capital and growth* (London, 1965) and Morishima, *Theory of economic growth*.

5 cf. in the context M. C. Kaser, 'Welfare criteria in Soviet planning', in J. Degras/A. Nove, eds., *Soviet planning* (Oxford, 1964).

6 cf. M. Kaser, ed., *Economic development for Eastern Europe* (London, 1968), p. 58.

7 cf. N. P. Fedorenko, in the same, ed., *Sovershenstvovanye planirovanya i upravlenya narodnym khozyaistvom* (1967); and Fedorenko's contribution to an attempt at a synthesis of problems of 'optimal functioning' of a socialist economy in his *Problemy optimalnogo funktsyonirovanya sotsyalisticheskoy ekonomiki* (1972), p. 14.

8 It is only right to point out the general attraction for planning theory and practice. On this point one will find illuminating observations in Herman Wold's recent paper ('Econometrics as pioneering in nonexperimental model-building', *Econometrica*, July 1969). He indicates the epistemological background of the controversy on the causal aspect in modelling. But – he argues – in econometric model-building the operative use of forecasting models has cleared up the haze around the predictive versus causal (essentially free of randomness) aspects of models; the celebrated proposition of a decade and a half ago of Tinbergen's *Economic policy; principles and design* (1956) – the proposition that if a model is to be applied for purposes of economic policy in terms of instruments and targets, the relations between instruments and targets must be specified as a (hypothetical) one of cause and effect – has become a matter of common consensus. This points to the growing aspirations of indicative modelling. Wold comes forward with the view that as far as the time-honoured issue of experimental versus non-experimental model-building goes, recognition is due, or perhaps overdue, for the 'integration' of both. This striking trend in development and thinking has naturally stimulated the normative planner's interest. (An element in this, incidentally, has been the change of the traditional view on the nature of normative planning, the new idea of its being too essentially an exercise in prediction – see on this our remarks on pp. 29–30 and reference to Melentyev.)

9 The collection of Marx's notes first appeared in Russian under the title *Matematicheskiye rukopisi* (math. manuscripts) (Moscow, 1968). The reviewer of the volume in the principal Soviet mathematical-economic journal pointed out that 'speaking generally Marx believed that a science reaches a state of perfection only when it becomes able to employ able to employ mathematics. Thus Marx foresaw the great potentialities which the application of mathematics opens to the science of economics' (F. G. Gurvich, *EMM*, 3 (1868)). The argument *in verba magistri* is clearly addressed to the traditionalist anti-mathematical schools in Soviet planning.

10 cf. G. A. Feldman, *Plan. Khoz.*, 11 & 12 (1928); Eng. trans. in N. Spulber, ed., *Foundations of Soviet strategy for economic growth* (1964).

11 See also E. D. Domar, *Essays in the theory of economic growth* (London, 1957).

12 For a short survey of the area of reception see Zauberman, in 'Economie mathématique en URSS', *Cahiers de l'ISEA*, Laboratoire de College de France, serie G. no. 30, 1972.

13 V. Nemchinov, in *Kommunist*, Mar. 1964.

14 cf. his article quoted ibid., p. 80.

15 Mathematically a system of simultaneous equations relating production and its final uses – the final bill of goods – does underlie the Leontief-designed input–output matrix.

16 'Sovetskoye gosudarstvo v opasnosti', *Byuletin opozitsii*, 31 (1932).

17 A. Zauberman, 'Soviet attempts to dynamize interindustry analysis', *Economia internazionale*, May 1968; also M. Ellman, *Soviet planning today* (1967).

18 cf. F. N. Klotsvog et al., in *EMM*, 1 (1969).

19 cf. B. L. Isayev, in *EMM*, 3 (1969).

20 Klotsvog et al, in *EMM* (1969).

21 Volkonskiy, in *EMM*, 2 (1966); E. B. Yershov, ibid.

22 *Our unstable economy: can planning succeed?* (London, 1966).

23 L. V. Kantorovich, *Matematicheskiye metody organizatsyi i planirovanya proizvodstva* (1939); G. B. Dantzig, 'Maximization of a linear function of variables subject to linear inequalities', in T. C. Koopmans, ed., *Activity analysis of production and allocation* (1951; circulated privately some years earlier).

24 cf. the statement by N. P. Fedorenko in the report of the conference– (*EMM*, 1 (1968), p. 144). See also below.

25 A. Nove, 'The problem of "success indicators" in Soviet industry', *Economica*, Feb. 1958.

26 V. P. Dyachenko, in *Vopr. ekon.*, 10 (1963).

27 A. I. Katsenelinboygen, et al., in *EMM*, 4 (1969).

28 N. P. Fedorenko, *O razrabotke sistemy optimalnogo funktsyonirovanya ekonomiki* (1968), p. 28.

29 Volkonskiy, in *EMM*, 4 (1967).

30 F. Klovtsvog, et al., in *Plan. khoz.*, 7 (1971).

31 L. V. Kantorovich/V. L. Makarov, in V. S. Nemchinov, *Primenenye matematiki v ekonomicheskikh issledovanyakh*, iii (1965).

32 S. G. Strumilin, in *Bull. Akad. Nauk*, 3 (1946). cf. discussion in Zauberman, *R. Econ. Stud.*, 16/3 (1949–50) and in *Sov. Stud.*, Apr. 1950.

33 The theoretical developments have been discussed by the present writer in papers i.a. in (1) *R.Econ.Stud.*, 39 (1948–9), (2) *Sov. Stud.*, Apr. 1950, (3) *Q.J. Econ.*, Aug. 1955, (4) *Economica*, Aug. 1962.

34 *EMM*, 2 (1971).

35 cf. L. V. Kantorovich/A. L. Vainshtein, in *EMM*, 5 (1967) and subsequent writing. At least the method permitted the authors to calculate the efficiency norm on some rational basis (their calculations yielded the rate of about 17 per cent p.a.). Traditionally in Soviet planning practice the value of the 'norm' has rested only on some rather arbitrary guess.

36 The debate is well presented (with sources quoted) in A. I. Katsenelinboygen et al., *Metodologicheskiye voprosy optimalnogo planirovanya sotsyalisticheskoy ekonomiki* (1966).
37 See Fedorenko, in *Sovershenstvovanye planirovanya i upravlenya narodnym khozyaistvom.*
38 Stone et al., *The model in its environment* (London, 1964).
39 J. T. Tou, *Optimum design of digital control systems* (London, 1963), p. 5.
40 Ibid.
41 The two fundamental works are: L. S. Pontryagin et al., *The mathematical theory of optimal processes* (New York, k, 1962); R. Bellman, *Dynamic programming* (Princeton, 1957).
42 S. S. L. Chang, *Synthesis in optimum control systems* (1961).
43 R. Bellman, 'Control theory', in D. M. Messick, ed., *Mathematical thinking in behavioural sciences* (London, 1968). R. Aris (*Discrete-dynamic programming*, 1964) restates the Principle in a somewhat different way: 'If you don't do the best with what you happen to have got, you'll never do the best you might have done with what you should have had'.
44 A. A. Feldbaum, *Osnovy teorii optimalnykh avtomaticheskikh sistem* (Moscow, 1966), pp. 97 ff.
45 V. Yefimov/V. A. Spivak, *EMM,* 5 (1972).
46 L. A. Melentyev, in *EMM,* 4 (1967). A note of caution may be sounded with respect to stochastic constructs in general, and typically the Markovian approach as the factotum in the treatment of the economic future. As Kelly and Weiss ('Markov processes and economic analysis', *Econometrica,* 2 (1969)) wisely remark, the popularity of the Markov model is due to appealing simplicity in the description of dynamic processes, to the availability of data for empirical analysis, and to its focus on the results as distinct from causes of change. But while it is generally recognized that the simple Markovian process is only a first and only a mechanical approximation, not enough effort is being put into probing into the validity of the simplest Markovian assumptions in the light of economic facts or economic theory.
47 cf. L. S. Pontryagin, in *Uspyekhi matematicheskikh nauk,* 4 (1966); the same and E. F. Mishchenko, in USSR, Acad. of Sciences, *Doklady* 4 (1969) & 2 (1970).
48 *Osnovy teorii optimalnykh avtomaticheskikh sistem,* ch. 7.
49 G. B. Dantzig/Philip Wolfe, 'Decomposition principle for linear programs', *Operations Research,* Dec. 1960.
50 See J. Kornai, *Mathematical planning of structural decisions* (Amsterdam, 1967); V. A. Volkonskiy, *Model optimalnogo planirovanya i vzaimosvyazi ekonomicheskikh pokazateley* (Moscow, 1967).
51 See V. M. Polterovich, in *EMM,* 2 (1968) & 6 (1969).
52 See T. N. Pervozvanskaya/A. A. Pervozvanskiy, in *Avt. i. tel.,* 7 (1968).
53 cf. T. O. M. Kronsjö, in A. J. Scott, ed., *Studies in regional science* (London, 1969).
54 The more one appreciates such studies in the field as, for instance, that by Jean Bénard, *La théorie du calcul économique rationnel et la décentralisation de la planification socialiste* (Paris, 1969), p. 37. Cf. also T. C. Koopmans/J. M. Montias, *On the description and comparison of economic systems* (Palo Alto, 1969, mimeo).
55 V. M. Zherebin, in *EMM,* 5 (1968), p. 756.
56 cf. Report from the plenary meeting of the Council (ibid., 3 (1969), p. 475).
57 The trouble with the existing information network lies not only in its failing to provide the sufficient amount of data but also, or primarily, in its incapacity for qualitatively handling the data accessible. According to Academician Trapeznikov, in some sectors 90 per cent of data supplied by the lower echelons to the planning centre, in Soviet practice, is useless for the latter's decision-making: this mass of useless information tends to block the circuit. cf. *Avt. i tel.,* 1 (1969).

58 cf. *EMM*, 3 (1969).

59 A. M. Rumyantsev, in *EMM*, 5 (1968).

60 Ibid., 4 (1967).

61 Symptoms of reconsolidation of the opposition to some tenets in planning theory and practice identified with a wing of the mathematical school seem to be observable at the time of writing. Thus Gosplan's theoretical journal recently carried a strongly emphasized article from which we quote (*Plan. khoz.*, 11, 1969), signed by a member of the editorial board, A. Bachurin: 'Those representing the mathematical-economic school sometimes simplify complex development processes of socialist production, and present them as an interaction of producer-collectives almost guided by market laws. Thus in his book *O razrabotke sistemy optimalnogo funktsyonirovanya ekonomiki* [On the development of the system of the optimal functioning of the economy], Academician N. P. Fedorenko (then head of the TsEMI) assigns to the commodity-money mechanism a regulatory function not merely in the production sphere but also in comsumption. In his view the commodity-money mechanism secures for the self-regulating producing units properties which permit the national economy to approximate to optimum. If, as the protagonists of the SOFE – the System of Optimal Functioning of the Economy – believe, the producer units develop according to the principle of 'self-regulation', the roles of the optimal plan and of the state in regulating the economy become ambiguous. Hence, whether the authors want it or not, they do suggest market-economy methods as a guiding development force . . .'. Further on the article criticizes the equilibrium price concept and remarks: 'Nor can one accept the SOFE authors' view that investment allocation can be based, under socialism, on price levels and relations. Such a point of view disagrees with reality and is very close to the stand in this matter of the "market-socialism" protagonists.'

The same journal carried in another issue (no. 12, 1969, signed by V. Sarykulova) a critique of the decentralization conceptions, identifying them with the school of 'market socialism'. Apart from social implications which, in the author's view, make this 'model' of socialism unacceptable, there is an interesting contention that it conflicts with the tendency for faster concentration in production strongly accentuated in the present phase of the scientific-technological revolution.

62 ASPR – *Avtomatizirovannava sistema planovykh raschetov,* published by the Akad. Nauk (Moscow, 1970). (The adjective used in the name has been explained to mean that the system cannot be taken over 100 per cent by 'automata'. The nuance is not easy to translate.)

Symptomatic for what I have described as the 'intellectual climate' is the present stand of the Gosplan, very naturally representing the continuity of the planning tradition. By the end of 1971 the head of its leading department (department of 'synthesis'), N. Zenchenko, wrote in its principal journal: '[the ASPR] should be conceived not as some kind of superstructure of "side-structure", or as an "instrumentarium" of planning but as *the* system of planning organically comprising also the mathematical methods and means of computational technique' (*Plan. khoz.*, Oct. 1971).

Academician Fedorenko in his report to the general meeting of the Economics Section of the Akad. Nauk expressed the view that the elaboration of methods of optimal planning and restructuring of perspective planning in this direction is likely to take about 7–10 years (cf. *Vopr. ekon.*, 3, 1971). It would however be a mistake – so he argued – to wait to implement mathematical methods till it is 'complete', if only because a method hardly ever reaches the stage of definitive elaboration. (Incidentally he indicated, as problems to which the highest priority should be accorded, those of the overall and local criteria, aggregation and disaggregation in models with hierarchical structure, probabilistic treatment of processes; also solutional algorithms.)

63 Fedorenko, in *EMM*, 2 (1972), p. 169.

64 Ibid., p. 171.

57

65 The theoretical aspects have been discussed by me at greater length in two recent papers: 'Statica e dinamica: mercato e piano', in *Programmazione e progresso economico* (1969), and *Reforms formalized,* paper submitted to the Eur. Econometric Conf., Brussels, 1969 (summary in *Econometrica,* 1970).

66 H. D. Dickinson, *Economics of socialism* (Oxford, 1939).

67 O. Lange, 'On the economic theory of socialism', *R. Econ. Stud.,* Oct. 1936.

68 cf. his *O socjalizmie i gospodarce socjalistycznej* (Warsaw, 1966); for discussion see Zauberman, in *Programmazione e progresso economico.*

69 Reference to views expressed in particular by F. A. von Hayek in *Collectivist economic planning* (London, 1935), and Lord (then Lionel) Robbins, in *The great depression* (London, 1934).

70 cf. his observations recorded in Kaser, *Economic development for Eastern Europe,* p. 211.

71 S. M. Vishnyev, *Ekonomicheskiye parametry* (1968).

72 Ibid., p. 172.

73 L. V. Kantorovich/A. B. Gorstko, *Matematicheskoye optimalnoye programmirovanye v ekonomike* (1968), p. 86.

74 The same, address at the September 1967 conference of the Scientific Council of the Akademia Nauk on optimal planning and management of the economy, *EMM,* 1 (1968), p. 146.

75 L. V. Kantorovich/V. L. Makarov, in V. A. Trapeznikov, ed., *Vsesoyuznoye soveshchanye po problemam upravlenya* (Moscow, 1971). There is also an issue related to organizational structure, i.e. of a realistic relation of aims and means in plan modelling. As far as indicative planning is concerned, it is reflected in the design of the latest French model for the 1971–5 plan as against that for 1966–70. The constructors of the latter stress the inadequacy of the convention in plan-modelling, under which the 'definition of macro-economic quantitative objectives is exaggeratedly privileged as compared with that of means'. Rather they adopt a method in which objectives, instead of being fixed a priori, crystallize in the process of elaboration of a set of plan variants – the process in which aims and means are correlated and the realism of the former tested against the availability of the latter. Cf. Michel Aglietta/Raymond Courbis, *Un outil pour le plan – le modèle 'Fifi'* (Paris, 1969), p. 5.

76 M. Tardos, 'The models of the central planning of foreign trade in Hungary', para. III, as quoted in ECE, *Econ. Bull. for Europe,* Sept. 1968.

77 J. Kornai, *Pressure and suction on the market* (1971).

78 Report in *EMM,* 2 (1972).

79 The problem broached is that of 'multicriteriality' – at present a subject of intensive theoretical inquiry in Soviet literature.

80 V. A. Trapeznikov, *EMM,* 2 (1972), p. 299.

81 A. M. Lyetov, ibid.

82 Report by S. S. Shatalin, in *EMM,* 2 (1972), p. 457.

83 cf. his contribution to the discussion in Kaser, *Economic development for Eastern Europe,* p. 323.

84 A. N. Whitehead/Bertrand Russell, *Principia mathematica* (Cambridge, 1935), i. 5.

85 cf. N. Wiener, *God and Golem* (Cambridge, Mass., 1964). Since these lines were written, I have found similar views expressed in a recent paper by Dantzig. He believes that the mechanization of data flows in the 1970s can be expected to pave the way to the construction of large models and effective implementation of the results of the optimization procedures. It is also his conviction that 'the application of mathematics to decision processes will eventually become as important as the classical applications to physics and will in time change the emphasis in pure mathematics' ('Large-scale linear programming', in G. B. Dantzig/A. F. Veinott, eds., *Mathematics of the decision sciences* (Providence, Rhode Island, 1968).

86 O. Morgenstern, 'Limits to the uses of mathematics in economics', in J. C.

Charlesworth, ed., *Mathematics and the social sciences* (1963).

87 Leonid Hurwicz, 'Mathematics in economics: language and instrument', in Charlesworth, *Mathematics and the social sciences*.

88 In *The Times*, 9 Oct. 1969.

89 E. A. G. Robinson, 'Recursive decomposition of stochastic processes', in H. O. A. Wold, *Econometric model building* (Amsterdam, 1964), in particular pp. 144 ff.

90 R. Bellman, *Introduction to the mathematical theory of control* (London, 1967).

91 Our italics.

92 G. Tintner, *Methodology of mathematical economics and econometrics* (Chicago, 1968).

93 See Pervozvanskiy, in *EMM*, 2 (1972), p. 300.

94 A. M. Lyetov, in *Avt. i. tel.*, 2 (1966). The author of this paper – on the gaps between the theory and practice – discusses the difficulties encountered in the build-up of optimal-control systems on economic criteria: especially the building into it of the feedback principle.

95 See Volkonskiy's contribution to Fedorenko, *Problemy optimalnogo funktsyonirovanya sotsialisticheskoy ekonomiki*, p. 33.

96 V. E. Shlyapentokh, *Ekonometria i problemy ekonomicheskogo rosta* (1966), p. 222. The reader will find more on this in Zauberman, 'The rapprochement between east and west in mathematical-economic thought', *Manchester School,* Mar. 1969.

97 S. Avgurskiy, in *EMM*, 5 (1969), p. 659.

98 Ibid.

99 Ibid., 6 (1972), p. 984.

100 Fedorenko, ibid., 2 (1971). An excellent discussion of general theoretic problems involved will be found in H. W. Gottinger, *Complexity and information technology in dynamic systems* (1974).

101 The same, at the conference on remote-horizon planning, ibid., 4 (1970), p. 630.

102 cf. E. K. Knox, 'A case for the computer', *Times Literary Supplement*, Sept. 1971.

103 cf. in particular J. Kornai, 'Economic systems: theory and general equilibrium theory', *Acta oeconomica* (Hungarian Acad. of Sciences), 6/4 (1971).

104 Trapeznikov, *EMM*, 2 (1972).

105 S. M. Vishnyev, *EMM*, 4 (1973).

Select Bibliography

BELLMAN, R. *Introduction to the mathematical theory of control.* New York, 1967.
—— *Dynamic programming.* Princeton, 1957.
BÉNARD, J. *La théorie du calcul économique rationnel et la décentralisation de la planification socialiste.* Paris, 1965.
BRUCKMANN, G./WEBER, W., eds. *Contribution to the von Neumann growth model.* Vienna, 1971.
CHANG, S. S. L. *Synthesis in optimum control systems.* New York, 1961.
CANON, M. et al. *Theory of optimal control and mathematical programming.* New York, 1970.
DANTZIG, G. B. 'Large-scale programming', in Dantzig & A. E. Veinott, eds. *Mathematics of the decision sciences.* Providence, Rhode Island, 1968.
DOMAR, E. D. *Essays in the theory of economic growth.* London, 1957.
DREYFUS, E. *Dynamic programming and the calculus of variations.* London, 1965.
DUBOVSKIY, S. V. et al. *Mathematicheskoye opisanye elementov ekonomiki* (Mathematical description of elements of an economy), Parts I & II. Moscow, 1973.
FEDORENKO, N. P., ed. *Sovershenstvovanye planirovanya i upravlenya narodnym khozyaistvom* (On improving planning and control of national economy). Moscow, 1967.
—— *O razrabotke sistemy optimalnogo funktsyonirovanya ekonomiki* (The elaboration of a system of optimal functioning of an economy). Moscow, 1968.
—— *Problemy optimalnogo funktsyonirovanya sotsyalisticheskoy ekonomiki* (Problems of optimal functioning of a socialist economy). Moscow, 1972.
FELDBAUM, A. A. *Osnovy teorii optimalnykh avtomaticheskikh sistem* (Fundamentals of the theory of optimal automatic systems). Moscow, 1966.
——/BUTKOVSKIY, A. *Metody teorii avtomaticheskogo upravlenya* (Methods of the theory of automatic control). Moscow, 1971.
GABASOV, R./KIRILLOVA, F. *Kachestvennaya teoriya optimalnykh protsessov* (Qualitative theory of optimal processes), Moscow, 1971.
GROSSMAN, G., ed. *Essays in socialism and planning.* Englewood Cliffs, 1970.
—— ed. *Value and plan.* Berkeley, 1960.
GOLSHTEIN, E. G. *Teoriya dvoistvennosti v matematicheskom programmirovanyi i yeye prilozheniya* (Duality theory in mathematical programming and its applications). Moscow, 1971.
HSU, J.C./MEYER, A.U. *Modern control principles and application.* New York, 1968.
HADLEY, G./KEMP, M. C. *Variational methods in economics.* London, 1971.
KANTOROVICH, L. V. *The best use of economic resources.* Oxford, 1965.
—— *Mathematicheskiye metody organizatsyi i planirovanya proizvodstva* (Mathematical methods of organization and planning of production). Leningrad, 1939.
——/GORSTKO, A. B. *Matematicheskoye optimalnoye programmirovanye ekonomiki* (Mathematical optimal programming of an economy). Moscow, 1968.
——/GORSTKO, A. B. *Optimalnyie reshenya v ekonomike* (Optimal solutions in an economy). Moscow, 1972.
KATSENELINBOYGEN, A. N. et al. *Metodologicheskiye voprosy optimalnogo planirovanya sotsyalisticheskoy ekonomiki* (Methodological questions of optimal planning of a socialist economy). Moscow, 1966.
—— et al. *Vosproizvodstvo i matematicheskiy optimum* (Reproduction and mathematical optimum). Moscow, 1972.
KOOPMANS, T. C., ed. *Activity analysis of production and allocation.* New York, 1951.
—— /MONTIAS, J. M. *On the description and comparison of economic systems.* Palo Alto, 1969, mimeo.

KORNAI, J. *Mathematical planning of structural decisions.* Amsterdam, 1967.
—— *Anti-equilibrium.* Amsterdam, 1971.
KRASSOVSKIY, N. N. *Teoriya upravlenya dvizhenyem* (Theory of motion control). Moscow, 1968.
—— *Igrovjie zadachi o vstreche dvizheniy* (Game problems on encounters in motion). Moscow, 1971.
LANGE, O. R. *U socjalizmie i gospodarce socjalistycznej* (On socialism and socialist economy). Warsaw, 1966.
LASALLE, J. P./LEFSCHETS, S., eds. *Recent Soviet contributions to mathematics.* London, 1963.
LITOVCHENKO, I. A. *Teoriya optimalnykh sistem* (Theory of optimal systems). Moscow, 1964.
MOISEYEV, N. E. *Metody optimizatsyi* (Methods of optimization). Moscow, 1969.
MORISHIMA, M. *Theory of economic growth.* Oxford, 1969.
NEMCHINOV, V. S. ed. *The use of mathematics in economics.* Eng. trans. ed. by A. Nove. Edinburgh, 1964. (Russian original *Primenenye matematiki v ekonomicheskikh issledovanyakh.* Moscow 1959.)
PONTRYAGIN, L. S. et al. *The mathematical theory of optimal processes.* New York, 1962.
Programmazione e progresso economico. Milan, 1969.
SHLYAPENTOKH, V. YA. *Ekonometrika i problemy ekonomicheskogo rosta* (Econometrics and problems of economic growth). Moscow, 1966.
SCOTT, A. J., ed. *Studies in regional science.* London, 1969.
SPULBER, N., ed. *Foundations of Soviet strategy for economic growth.* Bloomington, Ind., 1964.
STONE, R. et al. *The model in its environment.* London, 1964.
TINTNER, G. *Methodology in mathematical economics and econometrics.* Chicago, 1968.
TOU, J. T. *Optimum design of digital control systems.* London, 1963.
VISHNYEV, S. N. *Ekonomicheskiye parametry* (Economic parameters). Moscow, 1968.
VOLKONSKIY, V. A. *Model optimalnogo planirovanya i vzaimosvyazi ekonomicheskikh pokazateley* (A model of optimal planning and of interrelations of economic indices). Moscow, 1967.
WOLD, H. O. A. *Econometric model building.* Amsterdam, 1964.
YEFIMOV, A. N., ed. *Mezhotraslevoy balans i proportsyi narodnogo khozyaistva* (Intersectoral balance and proportions of national economy). Moscow, 1969.
ZAUBERMAN, A. *Aspects of planometrics.* London, 1967.
—— *Mathematical theory in Soviet planning.* London, 1975.

Addenda

ELLMAN, *Soviet planning today.* Cambridge, 1971.
HARDT, J. P. et al., eds. *Mathematics and computers in Soviet planning.* New Haven, 1967.
VALTUK, H. K. K. et al., eds. *Problemy modelirovanya narodnogo khozyaistva.* Novosibirsk, 1973.
VILKAS, V. *Matematicheskiye metody v sotsyalnyky naukakh.* Vilna, 1974.
VOLKONSKIY, V. A. *Printsipy optimalnogo planirovanya,* Moscow, 1974.
WILES, P. *The political economy of socialism.* Oxford, 1962.
ZAUBERMAN, A. *Topics in differential games* (forthcoming).

Note: For a more extensive bibliography see my forthcoming *Mathematical theory in Soviet planning.*

Periodicals

Avtomatika i telemekhanika (Automation and telemechanics)
Byuletin Akademii Nauk (Bulletin of the USSR Academy of Sciences)
Cahiers de l'Institut des Sciences Economiques Appliquées
Doklady Nauk Akademii Nauk SSSR (Reports of the USSR Academy of Sciences)
Econometrica
Ekonomika i matematicheskiye metody (Economics and mathematical methods)
Kommunist
Kyklos
Operations Research
Optimalnoye planirovanye (Optimal planning)
Planovoye khozyaistvo (Planned economy)
Voprosy ekonomiki (Problems of the economy)